Voices from the Bible

Volume One

An Anthology of Single-Character Plays

Rev. Kenneth W. Lee

Copyright © 2020 by **Kenneth W. Lee**

All rights reserved. No part of this publication may be reproduced, distributed or transmitted in any form or by any means, without prior written permission.

Wentzville, MO 63385

Publisher's Note: This is a work of fiction. Names, characters, places, and incidents are a product of the author's imagination. Locales and public names are sometimes used for atmospheric purposes. Any resemblance to actual people, living or dead, or to businesses, companies, events, institutions, or locales is completely coincidental.

Book Layout © 2017 BookDesignTemplates.com
Book editing and formatting by Jeanne Felfe
Cover by Cyn Watson

Voices from the Bible/ Kenneth W. Lee. -- 1st ed.
ISBN 9798698288077

Dedication

King David had his group of "Mighty Men" who supported him while he ran from King Saul. They fought to protect him because they believed in him. I dedicate this anthology to my own band of Mighty Men without whom Ken Lee Ministries could not have happened. Gentlemen, you taught me what a godly man should look like.

Bob Wise, formerly of Brockton, MA
Bill D. Dillard of Yukon/Mustang, OK
Mark Muirhead of North Carolina and Jamaica
Martin Perryman of Oklahoma City, OK
Bob Harris of Shrewsbury, PA
Dick Sochaki of Sterling Heights, MI

Ken Lee as The Roman

Contents

Foreword from the Author ix

The Full Length Plays for Men 1

The Roman 3

Barnabas, The Encourager 17

To Be a King A play in two acts 31

Merry Christmas, Shoemaker 47

Jonah, The Reluctant Missionary 63

Joseph, The Carpenter 73

Short Single-Character Plays Written for Men 85

Jedidiah, The Man Who Found Him 87

Melchior, The Man Who Saw His Star 91

Micah, The Man Who Made Room 95

Boy, The Young Man Who Served Him 99

Simeon, The Man Who Recognized Him 105

Lazarus, The Man Who Died 109

Orem, The Man Who Welcomed Him 115

Seth, The Man Who Watched Him Die 119

Judas Iscariot, The Man Who Betrayed Him 123

Simon Peter, The Man Who Repented 129

Octavian, The Man Who Guarded the Tomb 133

Thomas, The Man Who Doubted 137

Mahalaleel, The Man Who Told People 143

Zacchaeus, The Man Who Climbed a Tree 147

John, The Man Who Outlived Them All 151

Zorak, The Man Who Warned Pilate 155

Single-Character Plays for Women 159

Miriam, The Innkeeper's Wife 161

Elizabeth, Mary's Cousin 165

Mary, The Mother of Jesus 169

Mary Magdalene, Delivered from Demons 173

Martha, The Sister of Lazarus 177

Bildah, The Cross Woman 183

Zelda, The Servant of Pilate 189

A Mother's Prerogative 193

Mary-Not-The-Mother..197

ABOUT THE AUTHOR... 203

YouTube Performance Links:... 205

Foreword from the Author

The Bible is a "Living Word" which means that unlike legal documents it is flexible and takes on immediate meanings and encouragements for each reader while maintaining its eternal content. The Word of God never changes but our understanding and interpretation of His Word must continue to grow and deepen to meet the everyday challenges of our lives. The Holy Spirit of God leads us into all Truth. A very familiar passage from the Bible can suddenly "leap off the page" offering an immediate and much needed revelation. Another day we may read that same passage and see something completely different. As we ponder His scripture, we begin to see that even in the most familiar Bible stories, God leaves out certain details, allowing the Holy Spirit to anoint our imaginations to see new and significant possibilities. Many character studies offered here include a reference passage from the Bible. Each dramatic dialogue printed here has been successfully performed in actual church services. I pray that many of you will perform the monologues freely, but even more I pray they will offer each reader new and exciting discoveries about familiar passages and characters. May God's

Spirit of Truth help us all "rightly divide" His never-changing revelation.

Performances of some of the monologues in this volume are available on YouTube (links included in the About the Author at the end of the book).

In The Roman, I included several musical selections to signify the passing of time. In all six of my full-length plays, I sang both original and familiar hymns for several reasons. First, music is a familiar form of worship in nearly all churches. Since drama as a tool of ministry can be radically unfamiliar to many congregations, music helps to "normalize" the production, thus helping viewers more easily understand its message. Second, the sound of one person speaking for thirty minutes to an hour (however excellent and dramatic it may be) can "numb" the ears of an audience. Taking a moment for a character to sing is a familiar format for American audiences who are accustomed to the Broadway-style musical. It helps to renew the audience's attention span while deepening the personal impact of the play. Plus, I'm told I sing pretty well! In The Roman, I found it difficult for Flavius to sing without breaking character until the end of the play when he becomes a new man, more in touch with his beliefs. In the video I was able to sing entire songs by cross-fading to clips of me in a suit. In live productions, I was forced to use short orchestral selections while I had a "memory flashback" with bits of dialog spoken over the score. If you perform the pieces without music, such flashback dialog should be cut.

Other pieces also available on YouTube are found in "Day of the Cross." That production includes Orem the Palm-waver and Simon Peter. The play also contained Thomas but for some unknown reason, he was cut from the video when it was uploaded to YouTube. A third play is also available, "Portrait of the Man"—most of my fans will remember that play. Its script is not published here since I did not write it. I adapted the dialog from non-royalty material.

This anthology includes a lifetime's worth of dramatic material. All of the scripts have been successfully performed and God has blessed audiences in forty states and three foreign countries through their use. My most sincere prayer is that others will see value in my scripts as study aids to better understand God's Holy Word, and that He may raise up a few young "Drama-Ministers" to bless future generations with their richness.

In Christ's love,
Rev. Kenneth W. Lee

The Full Length Plays for Men

The Roman

My name is Flavius Lucius, centurion in his majesty's army, assigned to Pontius Pilate, Governor of Syria. I have been commanded by my Lord to tell you what I know of the man, Jesus. I must warn you; I am not a man accustomed to public speeches. I am normally a man of few words ... but those words mean something, and I am not used to being ignored. Understood? Just standing here before a group of undisciplined civilians like you ... well, just look at you. Sloppy. Weak. Some of you look as if you're about to be thrown to the lions. Some of you look as if you deserve to be. By the gods, some of you look as if you already have been! *(Laughs)*

Let me tell you this Jesus was not a weak man. Certainly not like I expected Him to be from His reputation. Not like most of you have pictured Him either I suspect. No, He was a real man, strong, intelligent ... filled with such ... power. You had to see Him to really understand. That's why I'm here. I saw Him. I watched Him during His arrest, His punishment, His execution—and even once *after* His burial. And believe me, this man was more than any Nazarene carpenter.

The night I first met Him, we had been sent to arrest the latest of the Jewish rebels, a Galilean who called himself Jesus, the Christ. Most of these Jewish rebels are weak, deceitful animals. If left to themselves, they'd eat their own young and roll in their own spit. Were it not for the disciplined control of Rome, they would have destroyed themselves long ago, but instead of gratitude, they repay us with rebellion ... as if we were the enemy. That night was just another example. We had to arrest their latest "Messiah." One of his cohorts pointed Him out to us, and we arrested Him.

However, it soon became obvious there was nothing ordinary about this arrest ... or about this man. I think I first began to realize there was something truly unusual about Him because of His eyes. Yes, it was His eyes. When we arrested Jesus, instead of fighting for His freedom, He simply stood there and stared at me. It made me feel very uncomfortable. There was something about His eyes that seemed to burn right through me.

One of His men, a big hairy Jew, grabbed a sword from one of the young recruits and swung it wildly at one of the Jewish priests who'd come with us. Cut his ear right off. Even before the rest of us could draw our swords to fight, Jesus grabbed the man's arm, made him drop the sword and then, right there before my very eyes, He picked up that Jew's bloody ear and simply stuck it back on that man's head! It healed itself, right there; we couldn't even see a scar! Then He turned and stared at me again. As if to say, "All right, I'm ready now. Well, what are we waiting for? Let's go!"

So, we took Him back to the Governor's hall for His trial. That man had such a regal, powerful air about Him. He was not arrogant, nor defiant, but He simply carried Himself with such—dignity. And authority! I'm sure onlookers must have thought Him to be a foreign king with all of his royal escorts, rather than a Jewish prisoner on the way to His death.

Now, I have never put much stock in feelings or emotions. Those are womanly, frivolous traits, which not only create weakness in a man but also complicate his life. The ability to act quickly and decisively in a moment of crisis is absolutely essential to those who wish to rule. Sentiment merely compromises a man's ability to act. A soldier who allows his feelings to influence his actions is a threat—to himself and his fellow soldiers. Still, walking back to Pilate's hall, Jesus strode erect and confidant, as if He were a king instead of a prisoner. Just watching that man, I couldn't help but feel—well I don't care if He was a Jew, I couldn't help but feel a kind of admiration for the man. No. No, not admiration. No, it was respect. Respect that deepened as the night went on.

We were instructed to give the man a thorough beating, and then take Him before Pilate. So, my men beat Him—thirty-nine times, with cat-of-nine-tails.

[Flashback as in video, this dialog may be deleted during live performance] "Not so hard! We don't want to kill Him right away. I said, not so hard! And hit Him lower, He's going to black out on you! We want Him to remember this ... every second of it."

We put a purple robe over His raw back, stuck a bunch of thorns on His head, called it a crown, and then took Him before Pilate for his trial. Even in His weakened state, that man was more than a match for anyone. He made no attempt to defend Himself before Pilate. He just stood there, quietly enduring the contradictory and poorly rehearsed accusations against Him. His quiet strength made

THE ROMAN

His accusers look absolutely childish. He even put Pilate on the defensive. *(Laughs)* I wish you could have seen it; it was wonderful! Watching that smug, pompous egotist outwitted at his own word-games. It was all I could do to keep from laughing out loud. In my mind I was cheering, "Go, Jesus! Get him! Make that smart-mouthed politician squirm!" *(Laughs)*

No matter how much I admired Him, however, to Pilate, Jesus had become a political liability. Therefore, he ordered Him to be killed. I had no desire to kill that man, but I am a soldier. I had a job to do. And I did it.

There was quite a crowd gathered to watch Him die. There is often a crowd at these moments, those who enjoy watching the blood, those who seem to savor each moment, watching death slowly, painfully invade helpless victims. They take bets on how long this one will last—or which of the criminals will last the longest. But then, I don't need to explain that to you, do I? That's nothing new for you, is it? How many of you have been witness to an accident, then find yourselves passing slowly by, craning your necks, straining to catch a glimpse of blood, guts, or gore? I've seen plenty of bloodshed in my years ... but at least I have never learned to like it.

I was raised with blood; I was weaned on it. My father was a soldier, as was his father. As a child, I'd been surrounded by suffering and violence. I'd seen more bloodshed by the time I was twelve, than most men see in their lifetimes. We boys were encouraged to attend executions. Father said it would build character. I remember as a small child, watching my own father cut off the hands of ten men, camel thieves, and watching them bleed to death, screaming pathetic oaths, swearing vehemently. And I remember standing there cold, unmoved, proud of my father and the power he held. I swore then I'd be like him. Well, I fought my way up through the ranks. I survived because I learned first to respect authority. Second, I learned to obey my superiors unquestioningly—and most important of all, I learned not to feel. Anything.

We decided to use spikes for His hands and feet. Straps were far too slow and risky. There must be no slip-ups, not this time. So, my men and I attached Jesus to the cross.

[Flashback as in video, this dialog may be deleted during live performance] "Line it up straight. (*He*

mimes nailing the nails) Now raise Him up. Hail King of the Jews!"

Now that Jesus was hanging on that cross, it was His turn to be stared at. I watched his face for glimpses of anger or desperation as the full reality of His pain began to sink in. I watched for His strength to turn to exhaustion, His resolve to turn to panic, and His confidence to turn to fear. You see, I've seen hundreds of men die; I know the scene well. Suddenly, Jesus raised Himself high, took a deep breath and shouted, "Father! Forgive these people! For they don't understand what they're doing." I had seen hundreds of men die, but I'd never heard a dying man pray for his executioners!

Jesus raised His head one last time toward the sky, and said simply, "It is finished." Then he collapsed—almost as if He had chosen that moment to willingly give up His life. But as He said those words, the already darkened sky became turbulent. Lightening. Thunder. An enormous powerful wind. The Earth shook! And as I stood there fighting against the elements just to keep myself erect, I cried, "Without doubt, this man was the Son of God!"

No, this Jesus was not a weak man! I had lived my life in search of ultimate power, and there on that cross I had seen power—power such as I had never thought possible. Power so intense it could move the Earth itself and turn daylight into darkness.

By the gods, what's happening to me? That sounded almost poetic. I'm beginning to sound like one of those hairless philosophers. Some of you may think my story ends there at the cross, but you're wrong! The story doesn't end there. Not by a long shot!

One of Jesus' followers made a deal with Pilate to allow Jesus' body to be buried properly. So, my men took the body down, and we delivered it to a quiet garden nearby. Some man from Arimathea had just had a new grave hewn out of the rock. So, after he had properly prepared the body, we helped him place the corpse in the tomb. Well, certain members of the Sanhedrin were still hot about Pilate allowing Jesus to be buried at all, so we were instructed to seal up the tomb as well as possible, then set up a twenty-four hour guard, to insure none of Jesus' disciples could pull off any stunts with the body.

THE ROMAN

Occasionally a few women would come by and weep, but for the most part everything was quiet. Dead quiet. I didn't spend much time at the tomb myself. I had to check on things occasionally, but it was obvious to me that however powerful this man had been while He was alive, He was nothing more than rotting flesh now, food for worms. I suppose I was a little disappointed. You see, I had secretly hoped He would win, that the power I had seen in His eyes would be strong enough to beat the system. But, once again, death had had the final word!

It was just after dawn, about three days after we buried Jesus that my men came—almost broke down my door. They were rattling on and on something about an earthquake and lights and a rolling stone. Well, I finally got them to tell me what had happened. They said there'd been an earthquake and that Jesus' body was gone, vanished into thin air. I made them take me back there so I could see for myself, and sure enough the tomb was empty, except His graveclothes were still there. I took my men to our superiors. They instructed us to lie about it. To say that Jesus' disciples had stolen the body. That was ridiculous! And it was an insult to my men. I know my men; they are not cowards! Nor are they women who would run from a fight. Nor are they fools who could be tricked. Those are trained soldiers, who are sworn to fight to the death rather than surrender their charge. But according to them, there was nothing for them to fight—unless you know some way to coax an earthquake into armed combat!

For weeks, I heard rumors that ... even now, this is embarrassing to say out loud. The rumor was that Jesus had come back to life again. The whole idea was ridiculous and a little maudlin. Still, I wanted to believe it. I had sensed such power in Him when He was alive, and if it were true, if Jesus had died and then conquered death—well, don't you see? That would mean that my search for the ultimate power had ended. If it were true, then I could finally have something I could truly believe in, something—no, *someone* to believe in. Someone greater than man, greater than all the enemies of man.

It was about a month after Jesus' body disappeared, I heard a rumor He was nearby, alive, walking, talking. I knew it was risky business, but I went to investigate. After all, I knew I would be able to tell for sure whether it really was Jesus, or just some elaborate hoax. I had seen Him up close.

THE ROMAN

I knew where all of his wounds were, their shape and size—and I am not easily deceived. And those eyes ... yes, I would know those eyes. I didn't want anyone to know I had gone, so I wore a disguise. After all, what if it was a hoax? I could lose my command for sheer gullibility.

I went to the place where it was rumored Jesus would be. There were already hundreds of people there, people of all ages, all classes—and there, at the center of that crowd, slightly taller than those around him, was Jesus. Or at least it looked like Jesus. If I could just get close enough. I moved my way through the crowd, pushing, shoving. I was desperate. I had to know! I elbowed my way through till I was only about ten feet from Him. Then, that big hairy Jew and a few others grabbed me. I guess they thought I might attack Him or something.

Jesus turned and He looked me straight in the eyes. Those eyes. They were His eyes! It was as if He'd expected me, and without speaking He held out His hands, His scarred hands, to let me see. Then He smiled and said, "Yes! It is I ... centurion."

He knew me! Had those men let go of me I would have knelt right there. I cried, "Master, if you can forgive the pain I caused you, then ... then I will serve you with all that I am!"

I can't remember that moment without being torn up inside. For though He possessed the strength of the ages, though He was in control of the Earth itself, Jesus put His arms around me—and He held me. He just held me.

Jesus is no longer here. He's gone back to be with His father. But I'm still watching for him, waiting for Him to come back to us, as He promised He would. But then, I'm sure you're waiting for Him too—waiting for a victorious conqueror to come riding into town after freeing his people from a vicious enemy. Yes, that's exactly what He is. A conqueror! A conqueror greater than Caesar himself!

Oh my, that sounded a lot like treason, didn't it? Ever since I've become a servant to Jesus, it has grown increasingly difficult to be a servant to Rome. I seem to be changing despite myself. My words betray me. Even my friends. One of my closest friends is that big hairy Jew, Simon Peter. Perhaps one day I'll have to resign my commission ... but, for the time being, I intend to simply enjoy the beauty of my discovery, the excitement of living a new kind of life. I don't know if a soldier can bring peace, but I'm going to try to do just that. I want to

THE ROMAN

live my life bathed in love. Love that is not based on weakness or dependency but true love that is based on true strength. Strength that is not afraid to be gentle.

Barnabas,
The Encourager

The man's handwriting is atrocious! I wish he'd let Tychicus do more of the writing for him. It looks like hen scratchings. Either his handwriting is getting worse with time, or my eyes are beginning to fail me ... but I refuse to admit that I'm getting older, so it must be his handwriting. Lord, it's almost as if he wrote it upside ... oh ... *(turns scroll upside down)* well it's not my eyes that are failing me, it's my mind!

(Reading from a scroll) "Command those who are rich in this present world not to be arrogant or to put their hope in wealth, which is so uncertain, but to put their trust in God who richly provides us with everything for our enjoyment. Command them to do good, to be rich in good deeds, and to be generous and willing to share. In this way they will lay up treasure for themselves as a firm foundation for the coming age so that they may take hold of the life that is truly life ..."

"Take hold of the life that is truly ... life." That's beautiful, isn't it? He is certainly developing a wonderful way with words. That was written by a very dear friend of mine, Saul of Tarsus. You may know him as Paul. He and I—well, I feel about Paul the way a father must feel about his own son. Watching him grow up in the faith has been as gratifying to me as it must be to watch your own son develop before your eyes. At least, I imagine it must be so.

You see, God never saw fit to grant me sons, yet I have become the father—the spiritual father of many. And believe me, if raising a child is even half as difficult and frustrating as it's been to disciple a young buck like Paul—then you can keep it! It's been hard work! Being a spiritual parent to a man like Paul is a lot like trying to force-feed a spitting camel. Shoveling good things into him is the easy part. Then you have to stand there and wait, hoping he's going to swallow at least some of it!

Oh, but I've enjoyed it though. I've enjoyed every second of it. In fact, much of what I've learned about God, the Father, I have learned by trying to be a father to others. You see, I never really knew my father. I was quite young when he died. He certainly left me well taken care of—financially—but I never really had anyone to ... well ... to do for me the things a father does. To teach me about life. To warn me about pitfalls. No one to rejoice with me in my successes, or to console me in my failures. No one to punish me when I needed to be chastised, or to reward me when I needed encouragement. I never had any of that. I was alone. In a house filled with servants, my only companion was loneliness.

Yes, we're old friends, loneliness and I; I have felt alone most of my life. Oh, I was surrounded by people—people who wanted something from me, people who wanted to be seen with me, people who wanted to use me. But there, at the center of those crowds, standing tall and pale, loomed loneliness himself, patiently waiting for me to realize that he was my only real friend.

The Synagogue was the closest thing to a family I had ever known. At least, people there acted like they knew me, like they were glad to see me. That's why I struggled so with the claims of Christ. Don't you see? I was afraid that if I became a Christian, I would lose what little "family" I had.

I had joined a crowd to hear Jesus teach once, and had even considered becoming a disciple of His, but He asked me to give away my money ... just give it away. It was too much! I couldn't take that risk. But after the day of Pentecost, when I heard Simon Peter preach such a powerful argument that Jesus was our long-awaited Messiah ... well ... I had to reconsider the issue. Jesus' claims to be Messiah had tremendous validity in light of the biblical prophecies about the Messiah, and in light of his undeniable resurrection from the dead.

I was afraid I would be banned from the Synagogue or even barred from sacrificing in the Temple because of my outspoken views. What I got was even worse. I got nothing ... nothing! No one argued with me. No one threatened me. No one even seemed to care what I believed so long as my money kept coming in. I felt used, ashamed, and alone ... more alone than ever.

It was Andrew, Simon Peter's older brother, who sort of took me under his wing. He'd heard of my public confessions of faith in Jesus; he simply wanted to help me understand Jesus' teachings more clearly. At first, he came to my home once or twice a week ... just to talk. I kept waiting for him to ask me for money, but he didn't seem to care about my wealth. We talked about Jesus, about the scripture. He was willing to listen to me ... really listen. He didn't just tolerate my tirades while waiting for his rebuttal. He really listened to me.

Slowly, very slowly, I began to look forward to our times together and became quite addicted to them. I even began to hope ... that he cared about me. Not the wealthy me ... just me.

Then we began to meet with others in small gatherings where we would ... oh, we would sing psalms and praise Jehovah for sending us the Messiah. In many ways, the meetings were exhilarating. The only drawback was that everyone seemed to feel both the desire and freedom to *hug* one another. Ugh! Those people were the *huggingest* people I had ever known. I didn't know how to respond to that. At first, people were polite and let me keep my distance, but when Andrew introduced me to his brother Peter, that man gave me a hug that would have strangled an ox! I thought my ribs would never be the same.

Then Andrew stood there trying not to laugh— and failing—and apologizing in the same breath. *(laughing)* "I'm sorry. I'm so sorry ... I hope you're all right. Peter means well, he just doesn't know how to do anything halfway."

Believe me, that was an understatement. Although, that was one of the things that drew me into the community of believers. No one seemed to be too good at doing things *half-way*. The commitment, the dedication of those people ... I'd never seen anything like it. Oh, I had seen zealots before but this ... this was different. There were people in those gatherings from every conceivable level of society—wealthy, poor, educated, ignorant, clean, dirty—but no one seemed to notice. And they shared everything. People who themselves had very little to claim as their own would over and over again give what little they had to those who were in need. As I saw their commitment and dedication to each other as well as to God, it slowly began to dawn on me why Jesus had said to me, "Go! Sell what you own. Give the money to the poor." His words came back to haunt me. "... and then, come. Take up the cross and follow me."

So, in one of those gatherings, I finally worked up my courage ... and I did it. I just gave it all away ... my houses, my lands, even my savings. I gave it all to the apostles and elders to distribute among the poor. I can't begin to tell you what happened at that moment. It was as if Jesus himself came striding into the deepest parts of my heart. And his easy smile and laughing eyes cut through the darkness of my loneliness. Jesus grabbed *loneliness* by the throat and threw him out, banishing him from my heart forever. I know that must sound foolish to you, but as I stood there in that gathering, I felt such a freedom, such a release of fear ... I felt loved. For the first time, I felt loved. It was just as if I were being born all over again ... only this time, I had a father.

From that day to this, *loneliness* has been a stranger to me. He still visits occasionally, but with God's help he will never live in me again. I promised God then and there that I would dedicate myself to a lifetime of befriending the lonely ... looking for the outcast, the timid, the fearful ... and then loving them into God's family. I decided I would do for others what Andrew had done for me. And so, I have become Barnabas, the spiritual father of many. After all, a new man deserves a new name. So just as Simon became Peter, and Saul became Paul, the apostles changed my name ... from Joseph which means "I want more," to Barnabas, the encourager. "The encourager" ... I like that! I like that a lot.

You must excuse me though. Right now, the "encourager" is in need of a little encouragement himself. I have been deeply troubled by something I just read in this letter from Paul. Apparently, there is some question as to our relationship. I where the rumor got started, but it is widely circulated that he and I had some sort of a big *battle*. Nothing could be further from the truth. We did have a disagreement about John Mark ... all right, it was a heated disagreement about John Mark ... all right, it was a loud, heated disagreement about John Mark. And the Lord has led us in separate directions, but we are dear, dear friends. I am very proud of Paul and the ministry God is building in him. I'm also very proud to have had some small part in the development of that ministry.

When we were in Antioch, Paul and I were chosen to go on a brand new kind of outreach. It was to be a "missions" trip ... we were to go preaching among the Gentiles. Oh, it was a sovereign move of God. Everyone seemed to sense God's directive, all at the same time. I had met and befriended Paul several years before that in Jerusalem. I liked him almost the moment I met him, but I couldn't for the life of me have told you why! He was a most zealous young man with the most amazing ability to offend people. I suggested he might increase his effectiveness if he learned the art of diplomacy—or at least good timing. Well, we became fast friends. We seemed to be good for one another. I seemed to be able to temper him somewhat—as much as one can temper wildfire. And of course, he had so many strengths that I could draw upon. It just seemed right for us to begin this new outreach together.

We also took with us a young man by the name of John Mark, a relative of Andrew and Peter, mostly to help with the luggage—you know, make travel arrangements, serve as messenger. Well that's the way we did it in those days. We trained a man first to be a servant, then we trained him to be a leader. I'm sure you all have your own ways today. At any rate, about midway through the trip, Mark got nervous, scared—all right, he got homesick—so he left. We were short-handed for a while, but we were able to manage.

After we returned to Antioch, Paul came to me. He was convinced God was going to send us on another journey. "Only this time," he said, and he tried to look me eye to eye, but he was about a foot shorter than I was so it ended up more his eye to my chest ..." But this time we are not taking John Mark."

[The actor must play both parts]

"Now, Paul ..."

"Don't you 'Now Paul' me. He is just too young, too immature to be much good to us."

"Yes, he is young ... and immature, but there's a tremendous anointing on him. He's such a tender, sensitive young man. He seems to honestly care about people. He just needs a little experience and discipling. Besides, everyone should be allowed to make an occasional ... mistake."

"A mistake? A mis ... He abandoned us!" And with that his nostrils started to flare, and his little round face turned beet red. "He's just too timid, too backward for the ministry. He seems to care so much about how people *feel*. We are not there to cater to their *feelings;* we are there to confront them with the claims of Christ!"

"Actually Paul, you would do well to be a little more sensitive to the feelings of others."

"Barnabas, the boy just has an annoying way about him. You have to tell him things three or four times before he finally understands. And he will never be a good preacher! You can hardly hear him a few feet away!"

"That certainly is not something you have in common, is it?"

"Look, he is just not ministry material."

"Why? Because he's not Paul? ... The boy got *homesick* ... he missed his home. That's something neither one of us knows anything about. You and

I, we have learned through the years to live alone, to make home wherever we happened to be. That boy grew up being loved. He grew up with a sense of belonging, a place he could call his own. Now are we to label him unfit for God's service simply because his ministry gifts are a little different from yours or mine? Actually ... I envy him his *homesickness*. At least he knows what a home is. Don't you see? He will be able to understand and minister to people that you and I will never be able to touch. And as to his qualifications for ministry, sir, may I remind you that every word you just said about Mark, had been said by the brothers in Jerusalem about you once—except for the timid part. Come to think of it, no one ever called you timid." Even he started to laugh at that.

"All right, Barnabas, I'll give you that one. I suppose it is true that no one would have ever let me preach, or even learn to preach, if you hadn't spoken in my behalf."

"Well then, why not give that same chance to Mark—the chance to grow, to develop the skills he lacks? After all, you and I are valuable to God, not because of what we can do, or because of what we possess, but because of who we are. And even more importantly, who God is enabling us to become."

We—um—*hugged*. Well it just seemed like the spiritual thing to do at the time. Then we prayed together for several hours. And we finally agreed. We agreed. We agreed that God was obviously leading us to enlarge our ministry. We agreed that Paul would take some other young minister with him, Timothy or Tychicus or Silas or someone. And I would take John Mark on our own *mission's trip*. As I look back on it that was the wisest thing we could have done. Don't you see, where once there was one mission team, suddenly there were two. And soon there were four and then eight. Yet all eight still beat with the same heartbeat. The heartbeat of Paul ... and Barnabas and Andrew and Peter and a hundred different others, who all left little bits and pieces of themselves in all of us. That's how it grew. That's how God's kingdom ... no, that's how God's *family* grew.

May I give you some advice? You can just call it fatherly concern from the spiritual father of many. Actually, it's not original with me. Jesus gave it to Andrew. Andrew passed it on to me, and I, in turn, offer it to my spiritual sons, Paul, Mark, and now you, if you'll receive it. The advice is fourfold. First, to those of you who are just coming to know the Lord, learn to pray. Pray. Pray that you'll begin to feel more and more comfortable in God's presence. So that you'll be able to take that presence out into a world that desperately needs His presence—and yours. Pray that lonely, isolated souls will begin to realize through you that only Jesus can fill the void in their lives.

Second, to those of you who have known the Lord for some time, learn to serve Him. Serve the Lord! Serve Jehovah with gladness. Wherever you find yourself, whatever you find yourself doing, whether men notice your service or not, serve the Lord. The kingdom of God needs its Peters and its Pauls, but it also needs its John Marks and Andrews—and even an occasional Barnabas or two. No one of us can be all that is needed, but together, each serving in his own way, we can stand in victory.

Third, to those of you who are called to lead God's people ... feed His sheep. Feed His sheep. Nurture God's flock with the Word of God. Spend your time building people, not things. Strengthen God's family with the living Word of God, and together they will become more than you will ever be in yourself.

And finally, let all of God's children preach the Word. Preach the Word, the living Word of God

Himself. Live the Word. Eat the Word. Breathe the Word. Let His Word fill you, and enlarge you until you will burst, sending small pieces of yourself into all those around you. Lord of the harvest, fill me, enlarge me, break me and send me.

To Be a King
A play in two acts

[Inspired by Gene Edward's book, A Tale of Three Kings]

Act I – King Saul
Narrator

To be a *King* is quite a task
and few have done it well.
Many men have tried and failed.
Some made it, but more fell.
Leaders come in many shapes
and each has his own way
Of getting forces to unite and
holding foes at bay,
But we can learn so very much from their
mistakes and crimes
And from the battles fought and won in
ancient, troubled times.
A King there was in Israel,

his given name was Saul,
A fine young man, this chosen King—
handsome, strong and tall.
He looked the part, he really did,
a regal, manly air,
Samuel knew him right away, "That's
God's choice ... right there."
When God chose Saul to be the King,
Saul's heart was soft and tender.
His father taught him to obey.
He knew how to surrender,
But once in charge, he seemed to change,
his knee no more could kneel.
He lost his love for people
and his heart grew cold as steel.
Saul's pattern for his rulership was not of
God's selection.
He chose to follow other kings, rejecting
God's direction.
A King there was in Israel,
his given name was Saul,
He started right, but then he changed
and soon he lost it all.

TO BE A KING

Saul, the First Israeli King

Don't look at me like that, I have done nothing wrong!
Nothing any of you wouldn't have done if you had been in my position. God chose me to be the King. And that is exactly what I have become, a King. And a much better King than Israel deserves, let me tell you. That is the real problem here. Israel doesn't know what a King is, how to *treat* a King, how to *serve* a King—how to *obey* a King. Someone must teach them obedience. You would have thought by now they would have become a bit more ... civilized, wouldn't you? *(louder)* Wouldn't you? Instead, they cling tenaciously to their old ways, their old tribal customs, religious rituals.

Don't look at me like that, I have done nothing wrong!

I only did what any King would do. Obviously from the looks on your faces, you don't know what a King is any better than they. Very well, I shall attempt once more to enlighten you as to the nature of a King. Please listen carefully this time. I shouldn't wish to explain this to you again. If you listen very carefully and use your brains this time, you may actually learn something. Although to look at you that would indeed be miraculous.

A King! A King is the central figure in any great nation, a rallying point around whom all of the country must gather. The King is the possessor of all of a nation's wealth. All good things are to be placed in his hands, all wisdom, all knowledge, all weapons, all power, all—all of the best of that kingdom. The King alone can determine the destiny of his nation.

What? ... What happens if he makes a wrong choice or a wrong decision? *(Annoyed)* That's impossible. A King cannot make a wrong choice or a wrong decision. For as soon as a king has decided, it is the responsibility and the privilege of his subjects to make that decision work. The king has merely to decide. It is the responsibility of his followers to pay whatever price necessary to see that what the King has declared should be, is in fact so! That is the real problem here. There are not in Israel enough dependable, talented, gifted people. Incompetents! I'm surrounded by incompetents! Servants who cannot obey simple orders. Soldiers who cannot even capture and kill a simple shepherd boy. Sons who make alliances with traitors. Priests who look at you with contempt and self-righteous smugness. Prophets who come late to battle! Incompetents. You're all incompetent! Dear God, how long must I cope with such stubborn, ignorant, intolerable ...

Don't look at me like that, I have done nothing wrong!

Look, I did not ask to be King. It was not my idea. Samuel. Samuel practically begged me to help. I was quite content helping my family, taking orders from my father, Kish. But God saw that I deserved better than that. He lifted me up out of that quagmire and put me where I belong—in palaces—surrounded by fine fabrics, jewels—God chose me to become the King.

Don't you see, Jehovah looked out at all the young men in his domain, all the gifted warriors, all the skilled intellects, all the musicians and athletes, and He said I was the best of all of them. God saw my abilities, my skills, my talents, my intelligence, and He said that I alone was fit to be King over Israel. Now that little boy thinks I will just step down and let him take my throne. Never! I am still the best Israel has ever seen. I may be older, but there is yet enough life left in this carcass to prove to everyone that I am still Israel's best. *(Yelling)* No one—hear me well, Israel—no one will take my throne from me! Hear me Jehovah, you will not ... Aah! *(wince in pain)*

Oh, Spirit, You must not abandon me now because of a few *mistakes*—no, not even mistakes. They were—*misunderstandings*. I had no intention of performing that sacrifice myself. It was the army's idea. I told them, "We must wait for the prophet, Samuel," I said. "God's prophet alone can perform the sacrifice for sin," I said. We waited for Samuel. We waited and waited. Finally, somebody said, "I don't think he's coming. King Saul, quickly! Perform the sacrifice so we can go into battle." All of those men, looking at me ... looking at me as if I should do something. It was unbearable. Oh, I knew what they were thinking. "Poor Saul! Poor Saul has lost his strength. Poor Saul is ruled by a doddering old prophet, too blind to find the battlefield. A real King would perform the sacrifice himself" All those men, looking at me, accusing me, taunting me with their eyes. "All right, all right, I'll perform the sacrifice. I'll kill the Lamb myself.

(Pantomimes killing the lamb. Then speaks to an invisible ghost of Samuel) Samuel? Samuel it's not what it looks like! Please let me explain. You were late—*(To God)* he was late—I had no choice. Look,

you can perform the sacrifice again. No one has to know ... Don't talk to me like that, I am still ..."

Don't look at me like that, I have done nothing wrong.

Hear me Jehovah, I have done nothing wrong. I have done nothing ... nothing ... *(Suddenly aware of the loss of God's power)* Where is it? Where has it gone? That—that feeling, that power, that anointing. Where is it? Answer me. Jehovah answer me. *(Yelling)* I am still the King. I am still the King of Israel!

Narrator

A King was killed in Israel,
his given name was Saul.
For though he started out with God,
how tragic was his fall.
For Saul could never say "I'm wrong,"
admitting human weakness.
He only said, "I'm good enough, I don't
need God's forgiveness."
God can give a second chance He longs to
show His patience,
But restoration only comes
right after true repentance.

A King there was in Israel,
His given name was Saul
He tried to reap what others sowed.
Uncommon? ... Not at all.

Act Two ~ King David
Narrator

David was a man after God's own heart.
God's mercy endureth forever.
He built a kingdom out of warring tribes.
God's mercy endureth forever.
David was anointed to be the king
Then for several years he lived in caves.
Saul tried to kill poor David -*But*-
God's mercy endureth forever.
David grew strong and powerful too.
God's mercy endureth forever.
His kingdom expanded
and prospered as well.
God's mercy endureth forever.
But David managed to keep his eyes fixed
On God's provision and faithfulness.
He never lost his servant's heart *And*
God's mercy endureth forever.

David made his mistakes, oh yes.
God's mercy endureth forever.
His passion and zeal
sometimes led him astray.
God's mercy endureth forever.
But David knew how to repent before God
He was willing to accept
the penalty for sin.
For anyone who trusts in God alone,
God's mercy endureth ... forever.

David, Second King of Israel

There comes a time in every man's life when he stops wishing his life away. He begins to dwell more and more on the ironic twists and turns of his past. You know what I mean, don't you? When you're young, time can't pass quickly enough. "If only I were old enough to go off to the hunt" "If only I were old enough to go off to battle" "If only I were old enough to marry" One thing after another. And then, all of a sudden it seems, your life is half over. Suddenly each moment is somehow more important, more precious.

Life becomes so complicated, so demanding, you find yourself drawn back into your memories, memories of simpler times—wonderful times. I suppose I've come to that point in my life. When I was a boy, it was my job to tend the sheep. Did you know that? I've never known for certain, but I believe my brothers stuck me with that job because I was the smallest. I had to tend the sheep day after day, while my brothers got to go to battle. I got to spend my time watching sheep chew ... then I had to listen to them tell me about mighty deeds of valor, slaying enemies, conquering nations.

I hated it at first and I hated those sheep. They did the same things day after day. They made the same foolish mistakes, endangering themselves and any others foolish enough to follow after. Oddly enough, those were the most wonderful years of my life. I grew up a lot, in a great many ways. Over the years, I actually came to love those sheep. I finally realized that they were just being sheep. They weren't deliberately trying to make my life miserable ... they were just doing what sheep ... do. I guess I began to feel a little of what God must feel, watching His sheep follow each other blindly, making the same dangerous mistakes over and over again.

TO BE A KING

Actually, it was good practice for being King of Israel, tending sheep I mean. Believe me there has never been a flock of sheep so slow to learn, and quick to disobey as God's human flock. And neither has there ever been a flock of sheep that needed protection more than Israel does. Not so much from some enemy as from itself. God, give me a giant you can see, and I'll fight him willingly. It's the invisible enemies, the Goliaths within—those are the battles I have never learned how to fight.

At one time I had a kind of a *pet sheep*. I called her Enoch after the man who walked off with God. Yes, I know she was a ewe not a ram, but the name just seemed to fit her. For some reason, I've been thinking about her recently. That sheep never left my side. She refused to eat unless I was in the pasture beside her. It didn't matter how thirsty she might have been, she would not drink unless I waded into the stream with her. If I laid down, she laid down at my feet—sometimes on my feet. She was dedicated but clumsy.

Once I climbed onto a rock, to watch over the flock. Enoch refused to stay down with the others. She kept bleating pathetically until I finally picked her up and sat her down on the rock next to me.

In some ways she was a real nuisance. I really came to treasure her, though, in a special way. Whenever I would call my sheep to gather them in for the night, or to move them to another field, Enoch would move first. The other sheep would see her move, they would get the idea and follow right along. All of my sheep knew my voice, but not all of them were very quick to respond to it. Some of them—some of them needed another sheep to follow—to be an example, then they would follow willingly.

Come to think of it, that's exactly how I feel about being King of Israel. I want to be God's *Enoch*. I want to be so quick to respond to Him, so tuned to His voice, so sensitive to His leading, that when the rest of God's flock see me move to follow Him, they will follow me. I am not the shepherd. I am a sheep like everyone else. People like to forget that, but my only value is to encourage others to follow the Good Shepherd along with me. If they start seeing me as the shepherd, or if I start to believe that I am somehow above them or beyond them—there is real danger there.

Poor Saul got trapped by that very thing. Poor Saul. He tried so hard to be what he thought he had to be—perfect. He demanded so much from himself, and then to hide his disappointment in himself he would lash out at anyone close by, his servants, his wives, Jonathan ... me. I loved him; I really did. But I don't think he ever believed it.

When Saul's spirit was troubled, you could hear his voice all over Jerusalem. Servants would run from him and hide. But somehow, when he bellowed like that—well, I couldn't help but see the little boy in him. The louder he got the more he reminded me of a little boy fighting against the world, struggling furiously to stay awake at nap time. I would sing him a lullaby or just play my harp, and sure enough he would begin to soften, sometimes literally fall asleep. I often thought that for all his bellowing, what he really wanted was just to be held for a while. The pressure on him was so great, trying to be God. Every mistake or failure was somehow proof that he was unfit for command. Half his time was spent covering up, ignoring his mistakes, pretending or trying to pretend they'd never happened. Then trying to invent some excuse or lie to push any blame onto some convenient scapegoat. As he got older, he couldn't keep the lies straight. Every time he told the stories, they were different. Saul felt such guilt over the things he did. He felt such tremendous guilt, and yet ... he never changed. He just never changed.

Don't misunderstand me, I'm not judging King Saul. I would be the last person in the world to stand in judgement on someone else's sins. God knows I have plenty of my own to make amends for. And if I ever do forget them, there are any number of others who would happily recount them for me.

How grateful I am to Jehovah that He is a God of mercy. If we all got what we deserved, few of us could walk away free. Least of all David, King of Israel. If anyone knows what it is to be truly forgiven, it is I. The greatest pain I have is that the penalty for my sin was not visited on me alone ... but on my sons. I see in them the real price of my sin. When I committed adultery with Bathsheba, it is I who should have died, not that innocent baby ... not our new-born son. I pleaded with God to spare him.

How could I have taken Uriah's wife? His only wife! It wasn't as if I were love-starved—I had nine wives, or is it ten? No, I had nine. Bathsheba is the tenth. And there are always concubines. I don't even know how many of them I own. How could I have been so selfishly consumed, so pompous, so arrogant, so blind? Dear God in heaven, what kind of man can do what I did? What kind of man am I?

I went into the tabernacle, grabbed hold of the horns of the sacrificial altar, and laid myself across it. I was determined that either the Lord would slay me as I was, sin and all, or I would walk out of His tabernacle a changed man. God would either change me ... or kill me. I honestly didn't care which. But God did not slay me. He forgave me. He changed me. He slew the Goliath that was raging inside, and I did indeed walk out of His tabernacle ... different.

But now, now I must face the consequences of my sin, try to undo some of the damage I have caused. That's why I could not bring myself to fight back against my son, Absalom. His revolt was just a consequence of my sinfulness. Can you understand that? Joab came to tell me of Absalom's revolt. He was ready to attack Absalom's armies. My son's following was widespread but disorganized. An early strike, Joab said, could scatter the forces and end the uprising quickly. But I could not ... no, I *would* not strike back against my son for something I had caused. Don't you see? I had made him what he was. His only crime was that he had learned too well the ways of his father. Can you condemn a young lion for attacking a wayward sheep? What else can a young lion be expected to do? Israel was God's kingdom not mine. And He must give that kingdom to whomever He would choose, even if it was to be my own son.

The power of man must be taken. It cannot be given or inherited. But the power of God cannot be taken. It must be given. Given by Him.

So, we left Jerusalem—myself, my wives, my armies. Content to wait upon God and try to accept His decision—whatever that choice might be.

God chose me.

And He did protect me. He slew the young lion and gave me back my throne.

"O, Absolom. Absolom, my son. My son. *(Suddenly louder)* Jehovah … give me another Goliath. An enemy I can see. A warfare I can fight with swords, or spears, or arrows. It seems that all around me are invisible enemies, spiritual giants that only you know how to fight. Teach me your warfare, God. Teach me.

Merry Christmas, Shoemaker

(Non-Biblical Character but the story is based on a Parable of Jesus)

Ah, the carols of Christmas. They're one of the best parts of the season. And even better to see the streets filled with fine young men and women singing them.

(After an awkward pause) Alright, Conrad, you came in here for a purpose. What was it? *(Obviously debating with himself)* I have no idea. *(To the audience)* Don't look at me like I am crazy. I don't care what my children have told you, I am not. I have been known to be a little ... forgetful at times. Although, I can't seem to remember when. Very well, I suppose my brain does occasionally wander

off, but that's perfectly normal for a man my age, isn't it? Well of course it is, Conrad. You are perfectly normal. But how normal is it to wander into a room and suddenly forget what brought you there in the first place? Wait a minute, Conrad, you've been doing that since you were thirty. That is perfectly normal. What is not normal is to stand in front of a group of people and carry on a conversation with yourself. You are a crazy old man. No, I am not!

(To Audience) Well, perhaps I'll let you be judge and jury on that. Oh, now I remember why I came in here. I want to tell you a story. A story about a shoemaker ... like me. He was a simple man ... like me. A rather big, hairy man ... like me. A big old, simple shoemaker with leather hands but a soft heart ... all right, it was me. But it's easier to tell the story if I pretend it happened to someone else.

You see last Christmas I was visited by Jesus, the Messiah. I mean, the Shoemaker, he was visited by Jesus. Now wait a minute ladies and gentlemen of the jury before you find me guilty of insanity, let me tell you my story first. I mean, *his* story. It's not as strange as it sounds. Although, when I see people react to it the way some of you just did, I must admit I have to wonder if it really

MERRY CHRISTMAS, SHOEMAKER

did happen, or if it was just some kind of spiritual vision—or a lonely old man's dream.

You see, I live alone. And I must confess there are times when reality and fantasy play musical chairs in my head. Ever since my Hazel died some ten years ago now ... Wait a minute, Conrad, has it really been ten years? Let's see ... yes, *(sadly)* yes it has. Well, ever since I lost her, I have been alone. My children? The children are grown. They both moved to the big city. They called me crazy because I refused to move off with them, but this is my home and I can't just pull up stakes and move every time they decide to ...

I'm sorry. I told you sometimes my mind wanders, but I think I caught him this time before he got completely away from me.

I really don't mind it though—living alone that is. I do mind it when my brain deserts me. But living alone, I rather enjoy that. The solitude, the independence—holidays are hard, but I have my friends, my neighbors, and my work. God has been good to me. And being alone has made God's presence all the more real to me. We talk often, He and I. I just talk to God as if he were a dear friend ... and sometimes He talks back. Now, don't get ahead of me ladies and gentlemen of the jury. I told you, let me tell my story first. I mean, *his* story first.

Well, last Christmas—actually it was two days before Christmas, the day before Christmas Eve—I was reading my Bible, just as I do every morning ... I mean, the Shoemaker was reading his Bible, when all of a sudden, he had a vision. There, in front of him, stood Christ, with his pierced hands opened wide, but with his face hidden by a cloud, or a kind of a silvery mist.

Jesus said to me, "Tomorrow, Christmas Eve" ... *He was very specific* ... "*Tomorrow* I will come to your door. Welcome me in, and I will show you a face for God that you have never known before."

Now the Shoemaker had never heard of this kind of thing before, a person being visited by Jesus Himself, but then he thought, "Perhaps even God gets lonely on the holidays." You see, God's children sometimes forget to spend time with Him too. They get so consumed with their businesses and their schools and their parties and their fun. *(Suddenly louder and angry)* Is it asking too much to take a few minutes out of their busy little lives to let an old man know that his children still love him? To show a little gratitude for his years of sacrifice and all the times when ...

MERRY CHRISTMAS, SHOEMAKER

Oh my, forgive me. I'm afraid my mind didn't just wander off that time; it completely flew the coop. But ... I believe it's back in its roost now ... at least I hope it is.

So, the Shoemaker spent all that day cleaning the house and shop, trying to prepare for the arrival of his honored guest. He took some of his savings and bought a whole smoked ham in case Jesus was hungry. Wait a minute, Conrad. You can't serve ham to Jesus. He's Jewish. Alright, I'll make it turkey. I set out a special pair of shoes, one of my best work, to give Jesus. Oh, and I set out the ginger snaps my neighbor down the street had given me. My, they are wonderful. The cookies that is. Well the neighbors are as well ... anyway, I went to bed early so that I could get up by sunrise. I didn't want to be taken by surprise by the arrival of Christ.

However, sleep seemed to evade me ... him. The old Shoemaker couldn't help but feel as if he were a little boy again anxiously awaiting the arrival of St. Nicholas. There are some memories that do not fade with age.

Christmas Eve morning dawned bright and sunny, although the Shoemaker's lumbago seemed to indicate that there still might come a bit of snow in time for Christmas day. I had a light breakfast and went all through the house making sure everything was in readiness. I even checked the doorbell to make sure it would ring. Well, I didn't want the Messiah to pass me by because I had a faulty doorbell. Then I sat down in my favorite chair ... I mean, the Shoemaker sat down in *his* special chair and waited for the Messiah to come. And he waited ... and waited ... and waited and waited and waited. My goodness. What could be keeping Him? Well, maybe

Jesus is not a morning person. I suppose that if I were the Savior of the World, I could sleep as late as I wished! Careful, Conrad, you're bordering on heresy now.

About half past ten, there came a knocking at the door. Well, it must be Him! It's a shame He didn't notice the doorbell. But when the Shoemaker opened his door, he found a disheveled old beggar, bent over like a man twice his age. He reeked of alcohol, nervously wringing his hat in his hands. The man asked if I could spare some food, or some old clothes to keep him warm.

"Well actually I am expecting ... yes, of course. Come in from the cold. Come sit by the fire, and I'll try to find something for you to eat."

MERRY CHRISTMAS, SHOEMAKER

Almost immediately the Shoemaker noticed the man's shoes, or what was left of them. They were barely clinging to his bruised feet by a little string and God only knows what else. The Shoemaker could remember being poor. He didn't like to talk about it, but he could remember pretty well the hungry days when his own father would leave home for weeks at a time, and then suddenly show up, smelling much like this man at the door.

I tried to pull together a meal, mostly the porridge I had left over from breakfast. Meanwhile the man rattled on and on about lost opportunities, bad luck, and people who had betrayed him. It was a familiar song. I had heard my father sing it many times before. But suddenly, the Shoemaker found himself wanting to treat this man with kindness, the way he wished he had treated his own father when he had the chance.

"I had planned to give these shoes to a dear friend of mine who's coming to visit today. In fact, when I heard you at the door, I was sure it was Him. But I think you need these more than He does. It's all right. He wears sandals most of the time anyway. Let me tell you about Him."

So, for the next hour I told him about Jesus. After all, where could he go? Don't look at me like that. After all, I had to listen to his tale of woe, he could sit and listen to me for a while. Finally, he left—but with a promise that when he finally got home, he would find a church to learn more about my friend, the man whose shoes had saved his "soles." Well, I thought it was funny ... he didn't.

Speaking of Jesus, I wonder what has delayed Him? Well, I'll glaze the ham—I mean, baste the turkey—with honey and add some potatoes. Surely, He'll be here by lunchtime.

About two in the afternoon there came another knock. Again, missed the doorbell. Well it is about time. Another thirty minutes and the potatoes would be hard as rocks and that ham—turkey—would have to be cut with an ax. "Welcome to my home, Your Holiness. I expected you much earlier—ooh! Wait a minute. Who are you?"

Instead of looking into the face of his Savior, the Shoemaker found himself facing a woman. Well, barely a woman. She was quite young, thin and pale. She was holding a bundle of so-called firewood she was apparently trying to sell. Firewood? It wouldn't have even passed for good kindling in most homes. She tried to smile and make her sales pitch, but her eyes kept rolling back into head as if she were about to—then she all but collapsed

MERRY CHRISTMAS, SHOEMAKER

right there on the porch. I helped her in and sat her in my favorite chair near the fire. As I retrieved her bundle of wood from the porch, I noticed that it had begun to snow. It was just a light snow, but I could make out the woman's tracks in the yard. Well, it was nice to know my lumbago still works, even if my brain doesn't.

It was obvious the poor woman hadn't eaten in God-only-knows-how-long. But all I had in the house was the turkey and potatoes I had fixed for Jesus. *(After a moment of thought)* Well, I'm sure He won't mind. He's probably used to much better cooking than mine, anyway.

The woman ate quickly, desperately, yet she kept asking if I were going to have enough left for myself and my friend. That touched me. Then she told me about her children. Her children? She was barely more than a child herself. She was trying to sell the firewood to buy Christmas gifts for them. They recently lost their father and poor or not, she was determined to make Christmas special. She hoped the children would stop mourning the loss of their father long enough to celebrate the birth of Christ her Messiah. She even tried to share her faith with me. We laughed together, and then she prayed for me. *She* prayed for *me*. I don't know if I

• 55 •

felt sorry for her, or if she just reminded me of my own mother trying to raise seven children in a Christian home mostly on her own—or if I really am crazy like my children say—but suddenly I found myself buying the firewood. Then I wrapped up what was left of the turkey and potatoes to give the children a hearty Christmas meal.

"There aren't any toys left in the house, otherwise I would—Oh! Wait a minute!" The ginger cookies. "Here you must take these too! Oh, they are delicious. The children will love them." She seemed much stronger as she left. "And a Merry Christmas to you. Don't forget now. If you need food, I have plenty more to share."

As I watched her walk away through the snow, I couldn't help but weep. God has given me so much. More precious to me than all the ham—or turkey—in the world is the memory of a Christian mother. "God bless that family ... and keep your hand on those children."

By seven o'clock it was already dark. The snow was falling, much harder than before. It was hard to maintain my faith that the Messiah would still come. I ... I mean, the Shoemaker stood leaning against the window, watching the snow pile up in the yard. What was that? Was it a knock? There it

MERRY CHRISTMAS, SHOEMAKER

is again. Doesn't anyone ever notice that doorbell? The Shoemaker opened the door, saw nothing and started to close it again, wondering if he was indeed losing his mind—again. Then he noticed a child huddled on the porch. Why the little boy couldn't have been more than four or five years old. He was trembling like a frightened animal, his little fingers nearly blue.

I wrapped him in a blanket and held him as I sat by the fire. I was sure the child would begin to cry once he warmed up and realized where he was. I never have been very good with children. Instead, he hugged me tight, laid his head on my chest and fell asleep, right there in my arms. I had no idea what to do. I was trapped. What was I to do now? I would need to take him to the constable's office in the village I supposed. Surely, they would be able to find the child's home. I decided to wait until his little hands were warm to the touch before we made the trip.

I would have gladly taken him home myself, but I'm afraid I don't know any of the children in our village anymore. Now that my children are grown—well, I guess I spend all of my time with other adults. But as I sat there holding that sleeping child in my arms, I couldn't help but think of how fragile and fleeting our lives really are. I must confess, it felt nice to be needed again. When my own children were small, I had no time to just sit and hold them like this. I was building a business. I never took the time to play with them, or to laugh with them or to just "be" with them. That was Hazel's job. Now my children have no time to spend with me. I was so determined they would never know what it was to be poor. But perhaps, I didn't realize how quickly they would grow up and how rich I was already.

The Shoemaker put on his coat, bundled up the child and took him to the constable. It was a shame he would probably miss Jesus' visit. But right then, the child's welfare seemed more important to me—*him*. And to his grateful parents. They were frantic, they had been searching for him for hours. We still don't know what made him wander off like that ... and without his coat and gloves. I hurried back to the house, but there were no footprints in the snow. I realized that if Jesus had come while I was gone, it wasn't likely he would have waited for me very long; on the porch—in the snow—wearing sandals.

Well—Christmas Eve had come and gone. Jesus must have decided ... not to come. Yes, it was just

MERRY CHRISTMAS, SHOEMAKER

last Christmas Eve that the Shoemaker finally gave up on his dream of seeing Jesus in the flesh. He chided himself for being such an old fool, just a lonely crazy old fool. I laid down and slowly ... mercifully ... fell asleep. In my dreams I could once again see Christ. Once again, I could see Jesus' wounded hands reaching out as if to hold me—but his face! This time, I could see his face. It was the face of the beggar I gave the shoes to. No, now it's changing. Now it's become the face of the young woman, and now it's the face of the frightened child. Jesus what does it mean? I don't understand.

(Recorded Voice of God) "Do not sorrow in your heart, my son, for I kept my promise to you.

Three times today I came to your door.
Three times my shadow crossed your floor.
For I was the beggar with bruised, cold feet.
I was the woman you gave food to eat.
I was the child who lost his way.
Three times I visited you today
And I sent the carolers to help you see,
When you gave to them, you gave to me.
My children know my voice it's true,
But the way I look is up to you.
My face, for now will not be known,

Instead in you is my glory shown."

I awoke to the brightest Christmas morning I had ever known. Last year Jesus gave me the greatest gift of all. He let me see His face. And do you know something? He looks a lot like me. And He looks a lot like you. And you. Or, at least, sometimes we can look a lot like Him.

Just last Christmas I learned that each of us may be the only "Jesus" some people will ever see. Don't you see, God sent that beggar to my door so I could finally learn to forgive my father and all those who had ever hurt me. Then He sent the young woman to remind me of how He had always provided for my needs. Finally, He sent the child to prove to me how much I am still needed in the world.

Well, you must excuse me now. I'm off to the big city. I have some relationship mending to do. I'm going to spend Christmas with my sons—whether they want me there or not! It's funny, I thought because my children were grown, they didn't need me anymore ... but, I've changed my mind. I still have lots of memories to build in those children ... and in their children.

MERRY CHRISTMAS, SHOEMAKER

Well, ladies and gentlemen of the jury, have you reached your verdict? Am I crazy? Please, don't answer out loud. I assure you that was a rhetorical question. What do you think? Did it really happen? Or was it all some kind of a spiritual vision or an old man's dream? Well, one thing I know. If I am dreaming, then let me forever dream on.

Merry Christmas to all, and to all a good night.

Jonah,
The Reluctant Missionary

I hate fish! I mean, I really hate fish. I hate the taste of it, the slimy feel of it ... and the smell. Phew! I have always hated fish as far back as I can remember. I remember once, one of my older brothers put a big, live flounder down the back of my tunic. It started flopping around back there. I couldn't tell what it was, but it was wet, slimy and wiggly. I didn't care what it was, I wanted it out. The fish obviously agreed with me. Finally, I got my belt untied and the fish fell through to the ground.

My brothers and what seemed like half the world were standing there laughing at me. They were always laughing at me. I was so angry—mostly at my father. He could have stopped them, but instead he was laughing right along with them.

"Heh-heh-heh-heh-heh! Don't be such a crybaby, Jacob! It was only a fish. Heh-heh-heh-heh-heh."

"Jonah—my name is Jonah." He couldn't even remember my name.

And that's when it hit me! The smell ... good Lord in heaven the smell. For weeks I carried that smell around with me in my tunic. Every time it got wet cats would follow me home.

So, you can imagine how I feel about fish now, after my "trip" to Nineveh. Please forgive me, I know I shouldn't be complaining; that fish saved my life. And I am truly grateful to Jehovah for His divine intervention--but He surely could have chosen some other creature to do His will. A sea-going camel maybe? How about a donkey who swims really, really well? A sheep with waterproof wool? Something—anything—but a fish. Just between you and me, it seemed as if—now I know this isn't true—but it sure seemed as if God was laughing at me too. It was as if He had every intention of rescuing me, but I imagine Him saying something like, "Sure, I'm gonna save the boy, but first—heh-heh-heh-heh-heh—let's have a little fun with him. Let's see, what does he dislike, really really dislike? I've got it. The smell of fish—heh—heh-heh-heh-heh—let's put him where all he can do is smell fish!"

What? Like you never had those thoughts about God?

JONAH, THE RELUCTANT MISSIONARY

So, He put me inside that ... whatever it was. Don't ask me what kind of fish it was, I didn't get a very good look! But I knew it was a fish. Believe me, I knew it was a fish. *Phew.*

Actually, I realize now that the only reason I was in that fish was because I didn't trust God. It wasn't that I didn't think Jehovah could protect me while I went to Nineveh, it was just ... well, I guess I was afraid God had forgotten my name. He must have decided I was expendable. Why else would He send a Jew to preach in a Gentile city? A very violent evil Gentile city at that! Obviously, God was only using me as a scapegoat. That's why I ran away. I didn't want to be sacrificed just so God could say He warned the city before He destroyed it—and me. That's what I assumed I was doing there in the ocean, just "floundering" around so to speak. I was sure I was being punished for my disobedience, being eating alive by a large, smelly fish.

For three days I was in darkness. I figured out later it was three days ... from where I was it seemed like an eternity. I was surrounded by blackness, covered in slime, strangely warm, yet totally helpless. I have no idea how I was able to breathe, or stay alive inside that fish, but God was obviously there with me.

I eventually came to my senses. God wasn't punishing me or playing games with me at my expense; I knew Him better than that. As I look back on it, I realize that He had been there all along—with me inside that fish. Just when I thought I was going to go crazy, unable to move, seaweed wrapped around my arms and legs, sea water dripping off the end of my nose, or dribbling down into my mouth—just when I thought I would explode with frustration, the presence of Jehovah would gently calm my heart, ease my panic, restore my hope.

"It's all right, Jonah, my son, I'm here." This time God didn't sound like my dad. "And, you notice, *Jonah*—I got your name right."

I was specially chosen by God to be the first "missionary." Missionary, that's the word I like to use. Coming from the word mission, which means I was sent there with a purpose, something I had to fulfill, and "ary" which comes from the word ..."ary"—well, it means—Actually the "ary" part doesn't mean anything at all. I just like the sound of it. A "Mission-ary." But that's what I was, a missionary, someone sent by God to preach repentance and forgiveness. He hadn't thrown me away. He decided I was ready to do something new.

JONAH, THE RELUCTANT MISSIONARY

When I finally found myself on that shoreline, I stood up and began to move my stiff muscles. I felt like a man just resurrected from the dead, walking out of a cold, dark sepulcher after three days. Hmm—that sounded familiar. It was as if I'd been reborn. I walked out of the ocean a new man. I had been delivered from that fish, just like a baby being freed from his mother's womb.

Well, I had learned my lesson. I would not disobey God again. So, I cleaned myself off as well as possible—*phew*—and headed for Nineveh, a little late, but none the worse for wear. The main thing that really bothered me was, why Nineveh? Now, I had never known any Ninevites myself personally, but I had heard the sailors and merchants talk about them. I had heard that they were really, really tall, and that they all had big fuzzy hairdos, and long scraggly beards. And that was just the women! And they all had webbed feet and claws for hands, and worst of all, they worshipped fish! Hah! I might have known!

I'll never forget how I felt as I walked through the gates of Nineveh for the first time. I kept looking at people's feet, to see if they were webbed, and at the ends of their arms to see if they would show their claws in public. People kept staring back at me.

Little children kept pointing at me and then cruelly pinching their noses. I was convinced it was a rude joke about my being "a smelly old Jew." Like we all have big noses or something. I figured they had probably never seen a profile as *noble* as mine. I realize now it had more to do with that rancid fish smell I carried with me. I kept waiting for them to … well, I don't know what I expected but it certainly wasn't this. Those people were—*people*. They were nice. Sure, their clothes looked a little funny. No, not funny hah-hah they just looked different—different than I was used to.

But their eyes. Their eyes were very familiar. In their eyes I could see the same hurt, the same fear of rejection, the same insecurities that I've always seen in my mirror. They looked every bit as afraid of me and my "different-ness" as I ever had been of them. Oh, did I mentioned that my skin turned white inside the fish? As white as alabaster.

I told those people what God sent me there to tell them. "People of Nineveh listen to me! If you don't stop your wicked, cruel, sinful … stuff, Jehovah God is going to destroy this city." Okay, so I'm not much of a public speaker. So, sue me. "Listen to me, people of Nineveh. Jehovah God, the only true God sent me here to talk to you and to warn

JONAH, THE RELUCTANT MISSIONARY

you. You must stop the violence! The way you kill each other, sometimes in the name of your gods—Jehovah God really hates that. And all of your pagan altars, altars dedicated to bull-gods, frog-gods, and even fish-gods. You must tear them down, people of Assyria—especially the fish god altars—He really, really hates them. You must obey Jehovah, put on sack cloth and ashes, and pray that He will forgive you."

Then, one of them, I think it was the mayor, stepped forward and asked, "If we repent and pray to Jehovah as you ask, will He then spare our city?"

I had no idea. That question hadn't even occurred to me. I paused for a moment, then replied, "All I know is that if you *don't* repent, He *will* wipe out your entire city. But Jehovah is a just God, and a loving God, at least to us Jews. Look, all I know is what He told me to say. God sent me here to warn you, so consider yourselves warned. The rest is up to Him."

Then I stormed out of the city and onto the nearby hillside, a place where I could watch for the fire and brimstone to fall. After I sat for a moment, that question bounced around in my head. Would God spare their city? It seemed ridiculous. Why would He forgive a bunch of vicious pagans? I didn't have an answer, yet I couldn't get the question out of my mind.

After some time had passed, I decided it might take a little longer for judgement to fall than I originally expected, so I built a vine arbor to protect me from the sun. There was this wonderful gourd plant with enormous leaves on it. I wove it into my arbor and sat down in its shade. All that day I asked myself. Will the Ninevites repent? I know what will happen if they don't—but what will happen if they do repent? All that night I waited. Nothing. Dawn came and still nothing. I couldn't believe it.

"God this isn't fair! Those people are going to think I'm a total crackpot!" And to top it all off, that beautiful gourd plant, you know the one with the big leaves, it had died during the night and the leaves just shriveled up. There I was with egg all over my face and absolutely nothing to shield myself from the noonday sun. Well that was the last straw! I kicked over that arbor and yelled, "I've had it Jehovah! Just kill me and get it over with. What? It isn't bad enough that you send me to the ends of the earth to preach to heathen Gentiles? It isn't enough that you strip me of my dignity, making me smell of fish spit? I'll bet the whole city is having a real good laugh at my expense. Come on God, I'd rather die right here than have to face those Ninevites again! Well, all right! Let 'em laugh! Let 'em all laugh, the Ninevites, my brothers—my father—and now my God."

Then God spoke to me, a lot louder than I expected, "Jonah, do you realize what you're upset about? You're angry at me because of the sudden death of a gourd *plant*, and in the same breath, you expect me to kill a whole race of *people* just because you think they're laughing at you. Which is more valuable Jonah? A plant or a human soul? I brought you to Nineveh because I love those people just like I love you. Surely someone like you, someone who knows the pain of rejection, could learn to serve and even love a rejected race."

He was right. He's always right. I can't believe I cared more for that plant than I did for all of those people. I had never thought of myself as being a "respecter of persons," but I obviously was. God forgive me. Then, it suddenly dawned on me that I had never known a relationship built on love alone. The only things I had ever "loved" were things I found useful, things that brought me pleasure, things that gave me comfort like the plant. In fact, the only people I really loved were the ones who were nice to me. Maybe that's why I was so suspicious of God. I didn't understand why He could love me when He obviously didn't need me. I thought all God wanted was my obedience, but He wanted more. He wanted my love. God demanded my obedience so that He could teach me how to love.

"Jonah, you really should have learned this lesson with the fish. I will use and bless—and love anything or anyone I choose. I'm God! I get to do that."

The fish, the thing I hated so much, was the very thing God used to save me. And the Ninevites, whom I once had hated, taught me how to love. God gave me years, wonderful years of ministry among them.

"Jehovah, I guess I have a lot to learn about your kind of love. You don't love whoever you find useful. You make useful whoever you love. Just as you were willing to love me, I'm willing to learn to love them. And as you were willing to serve me, I'm willing now to serve you by serving them."

Joseph, The Carpenter

"Son always remember, the path of the righteous is not always well lit ... but it is always well planned."

Those were my father's last words to me. I've never forgotten them. They have strengthened me through some pretty painful times. Not bad philosophy coming from an old Galilean carpenter, huh?

Papa ... Papa never had very much. This ratty old shawl. He wore it always; I think it was a gift from Mama. An old work bench, a few well-worn tools, and all the wood chips you could eat. It's strange. I used to look at his hands, large, swollen knuckles, callouses, splinters ... I was afraid of them, afraid to touch him, or let him touch me. Now ... now my hands look more like his every day. No, Papa didn't have much to leave me, but he taught me a trade. He showed me what it really means to be a man, and he taught me to serve and obey Jehovah God. Hmm. On second thought, my father did have much to leave me. I only hope I will have as much to leave for my eldest son.

My eldest son ... well, actually I suppose he's not my son, not physically. But he is my son in every way that counts. I know someday I'll have to give him up, *(suddenly louder)* but then doesn't any father have to give up his son sometime? For now, he's mine and I intend to teach him all that my father taught me. *(As if waking up)* I'm sorry. I didn't mean to speak so loudly ... or spit so far.

It's just that we waited so long for him, Mary and I. Oh, Mary—Mary is my wife—except she wasn't *yet* my wife when—not that she did anything that— or that we did anything that you ... I think I better start at the beginning. Words are clumsy things for me. And you all have very dirty minds.

Mary and I were engaged. Our fathers had just concluded the arrangements. We were so happy. I had fallen in love with Mary when we were both children. Now, I know most young men ... most young men are always looking at girls—and then prophesying. Predicting which would make good wives, which would make good servants, and which would make good ... well, you know how young men's minds work. It is amazing how some

JOSEPH, THE CARPENTER

things never change. But with Mary, it was different. As soon as I met her, I knew that she was all I wanted. Don't ask me how I knew. I just knew.

I went into my father, now mind you I was only fifteen years old at the time, and I said, "Father *(voice cracks)!*" My voice was still changing. "Father! I wish to marry Jacob's daughter, Mary!" He tried so hard not to laugh—but Mary was only six years old at the time.

I'll never forget, Papa finally gained his composure and he started to nod. Papa always nodded when he didn't know what to say. *(Nodding)* "In due time, son. In due time. Someday, someday you'll meet a nice Jewish girl, you'll get married, you'll settle down, you'll make me Grandpapa. So, what's your hurry? I'm too young to be Grandpapa. So, wait a little. Wait a little."

I think he expected me to change my mind before I reached marrying age. But I didn't change my mind. On my twenty-second birthday I marched into him again and said, "Father! Father I wish to marry Jacob's daughter, Mary!" This time he could not refuse me. I was head and shoulders taller than he was and my voice didn't crack.

So, he contacted her father; they bartered a little, and it was done. She was to be mine. That's when ... that's when she told me she was going to have a baby. We had just started to plan our wedding and she tells me she's going to have a ... Then, to make matters worse she tells me that the baby is not just a baby. Oh, no. She tells me the baby is actually the Messiah and that she has been chosen to give Him birth. The baby was sired by Jehovah-Jireh Himself. Oy veh!

Now, it was obvious to me that she really believed what she was telling me. I think that scared me even worse. I mean, I'm a carpenter. I'm not a theologian. She quoted from the holy scrolls a passage about a virgin conceiving, but they were just words. I know what happens to a woman in Galilee who is found to be with child before her wedding. She could be stoned. And believe me, in a little town like Nazareth, rumors fly very quickly. Frankly I was so concerned about Mary's life being in danger once word got out that I decided ... I decided I didn't care where the baby came from. I decided I would take Mary away and try to build a new life for ourselves. I was a pretty fair carpenter, even then. I could probably make a modest living for us. The only problem was ... where? Where could we go to escape the gossips?

JOSEPH, THE CARPENTER

I was in my shop, working on an old ox-yoke, taking out all my frustrations on that defenseless piece of wood. All of a sudden, a strange shiver ran through me. Everything got suddenly quiet. I felt almost as if someone were looking over my shoulder. I turned and was almost blinded by an incredible light. A voice spoke to me out of the light. The voice said, "Don't be afraid. Don't be afraid of me, don't be afraid of things that you don't understand. Mary," ... *He called her by name* ... "Mary has not been unfaithful to you. The child she will bear is the Son of the Most High God. He will rescue your nation ... the entire world from their sin."

As my eyes began to adjust to the light a little bit, I could make out the form of a man. He seemed to be standing above the floor—a few cubits above the floor. His clothes were bright and glowing, and his face burned with white-hot fire. We talked for some time about the baby, about our future—well, actually he spent most of the time telling me not to fear what I didn't understand. Then, it was just as if I woke up abruptly. There was my bench. There was the ox-yoke, but the man was gone. I couldn't have been dreaming; it was mid-day. It must have really happened. I was visited by an angel ... or ... something.

No, but that's heresy. Could an angel appear to a carpenter? I thought they only showed themselves to prophets or priests—or at least rabbis. I ran to find my papa. Papa would know. He never had much education, but he was the wisest and most spiritual man I'd ever known. Normally, he would have been with me there in the shop, but that morning he'd had a tightness in his chest and seemed to be short of breath. I insisted he stay in bed.

I went in, woke him up and told him what I thought had just happened to me. I'll never forget the look on his face. He was confused, but not shaken. Papa insisted on getting up and he started to nod. I knew what that meant.

(Nodding as before) "Son ... I don't understand what is happening to you. Jehovah may be speaking to you. You've become quite a fine man, stable, obedient, bright. On the other hand, I have never heard of God speaking directly to common men—except for Uncle Mordecai—who also sees flying camels in the temple! Son, I cannot tell you what it means. But there is one thing I can tell you. You must trust in God. You are His. Son always remember, the path of the righteous is not always well lit ... but it is always well planned."

JOSEPH, THE CARPENTER

Sometime during the night that night Papa went to join his ancestors ... but his words went with me, first to Bethlehem, then into Egypt and finally back here to Nazareth. God has been faithful to us. He has miraculously protected us from harsh weather, unseen robbers, even from that madman, Herod. Through all of our confusion, fear, and disbelief, God never gave up on us. He taught us to truly trust in Him, not in the things around us. Not even in the people ... *(Suddenly thinking of Papa)* ... not even in the people around us. I only hope I will be able to teach that same lesson to all of my sons.

As far as the actual birth of Jesus, I don't need to tell you that story, do I? Some of you know the story as well as I do. It all happened so quickly. The hurried trip to Bethlehem, the stable, the manger—and the shepherds. Phew! And that star. That huge star appeared twice. Did you know that? The first time was on the night of our son's birth, but after Jesus was born, we stayed in Bethlehem. I started doing odd jobs around town and eventually opened my own shop. Finally, I was able to build us a home near town.

It was somewhere around our son's second birthday and we had just settled in for the night when there came visitors, apparently from some great distance away. They asked me where they might find the Messiah. I said, "Why would you seek Him here?" They said they had seen His star some two years ago and had come to Jerusalem on the basis of the prophecies about the Messiah. But once they got to Jerusalem—where? It was then that the star reappeared and led them here. I looked up and there was that star, shining bright as ever right over our house. Oy veh!

Well, I knew because of the star that God had led them here, so I let them in—reluctantly. I was still uncomfortable with the whole situation. Once inside, I discovered that those men were kings or rulers or something. Those grown men bowed before our young son and gave him gifts. Hmpf! Gifts. Gifts too expensive for a child his age.

But somehow, seeing them together like that ... it began to dawn on me. Would I be capable of raising and training a young ... well ... a young king? After the men left, we went back to bed, but I was wakened by a dream that my son was in great danger. So, I gathered my family together and we left that very night for Egypt. We stayed in Egypt for several years, until I was certain Herod had died. Then I brought my family back here, to Nazareth. I

JOSEPH, THE CARPENTER

wanted Jesus to grow up here, in my hometown, among people I knew.

Jesus has become quite a helper to me now. His work ... *(suddenly softer as if Jesus might overhear)* ... His work is nearly as good as mine. But don't tell Him I said so! Not yet. His time will come soon enough.

I have a sign in my shop that says, "My yokes fit well." Jesus keeps teasing me. He says he's going to put up a sign, "My yokes fit better." I'm not at all certain we're talking about the same kind of yoke though. He's a fine young boy—no, no He's not. He's a fine young man. A strong—a strong young man. His hands! His hands are so large and strong that you could drive a spike through those hands, and he wouldn't even ... *(Staggering and holding his arm in pain)*

Oh! Oh, I seem to have a pain in my arm. I'll be all right. The pain will pass soon. It always does. You would think I'd be used to a little pain by now, wouldn't you? Oh my! Perhaps I'd better stop and let Jesus mind the shop for me. He really does do a good job. I have at least trained Him well. I only wish I had more to offer Him, but I've already given Him my most cherished possession, the inheritance of an eldest son. As my first child, he will inherit all that I have and all I've received from my fathers. I only hope that James, our first natural-born son, will one day understand why he could not receive the legacy. But from the first moment I saw Jesus, I knew. I knew. I knew that He was indeed the Messiah, the Savior of the World, the one all Israel has prayed for for generations.

On his twelfth birthday, we took Him to the temple in Jerusalem, as was our custom. That particular year, several families traveled together, and we all had our own responsibilities and errands, and ... well ... in all the confusion—we lost Jesus. I thought He was with Mary. She thought He was with me. We began to retrace our steps to look for Him. We found Him in Jerusalem, in the Temple! For three days, Jesus sat with elders, scribes, Pharisees, talking with them, asking questions, conversing with them about the Holy Scrolls. And, if I know Jesus, he was probably trying to teach those old goats a thing or two about God! They were quite impressed, both with His wisdom, and with His knowledge of scripture. They even asked who His teacher was. I nearly told them.

One of the men traveling with us suggested that perhaps we should leave him there, in the temple with the priests. That way they could train him properly in the Holy Scrolls. But I said no. "No! No, if God had wanted Him to be a Levite, He would have had Him born to a Levite. God gave Him to me." I began to realize then that just as Mary had been chosen to give Him birth, I had been chosen to give Him guidance. I must see to His training in good deeds, His instruction in righteousness and holiness. I began to realize that Jesus was as much mine as He was Mary's.

I shall never forget carrying Him into the Temple to celebrate His bris. I presented Him to the priest, made the proper sacrifice, and recited the Pidyon Haben. I shall never forget my pride as I raised Him high and prayed, "Blessed are you, Lord our God, Father of Israel. Accept this sacrifice in redemption of this, my firstborn son. And may it be your will that as He has entered the redemption of the firstborn, may He grow in grace, and stature, and in favor with God and men. And may His name be called in Israel, Jesus—the son of Joseph, a carpenter."

How ironic, that I should redeem the one who would one day redeem me.

"Little one, always remember. The path of the righteous is not always well lit … but it is always well planned.

Short Single-Character Plays Written for Men

Jedidiah,
The Man Who Found Him

Scripture reference~ Luke 2:15~20

It were a light! I'm tellin' ya, it were a light! A great, great biggun! I ain't never see'd a star that big afore. Ya see what happen'd was this. We's all out on the hillside. All of us ... Aaron and Jethro and Arphaxad and Nadab and Doodad and Rebob and Jimbob ... like I said, all of us. My name is Jedidiah by the way. I'm the good-lookin' one. My momma said when I was borned I jest looked like a Jedidiah. Ain't got no idea what that means though.

Anyhow, it were real quiet on the hillside. Nadab was a playin' his flute, not real loud like he used ta but real soft like. And quicker than a lady bug can fly up your nose, Zingo! There they was. They was this big old star and angels all over the sky jest a sangin' ta beat the band. They was all dressed in white with gold crowns. Whoo boy was they perdy!

I was a fixin' ta run. No, I weren't afeared or nothin', but I was a thankin', "Jedidiah, you know nobody's is gonna believe we see'd angels unless we had us some reliable witnesses." So, I's fixin' ta run to find somebody people wouldn't laugh at to see them angels and the star ... but I couldn't move. All's I could do were stand there and listen ta them boys sang! And I mean they sung their little wings off. "Glory ta God! Glory ta God in the Highust! And on earth let there be peace and good wee-ull to me-un!" Jest like that ... 'cept they sounded good. Yeah, I may be good-lookin' but I sang like a crow!

Then this one real big angel told us ta go down to Bethlehem and find us a baby in a manger. Yep, that's shore enuf what he said. He said, "In a manger," that's where we'd find the baby. He said He was the Savior of the world ... not the angel, the baby ... I mean the angel said it, not the baby, but it was the baby what were the Savior, not the angel ... You folks getting' all this? Ya'll lookin' at me like I got somethin' stuck ta my teeth.

JEDIDIAH, THE MAN WHO FOUND HIM

But ya know somethin'? We run down to Bethlehem and that's right where we found Him ... the baby not the angel. He was there in the stable, His mama Mary, Joseph His daddy, and that sweet baby. There they was sleepin' in a manger. I mean the baby was sleeping in the manger, not Mary and Joseph ... well actually His Mama was still layin' in the hay but the baby was in the manger. Oh, he were a goodun, that's fer sure!

Only now we cain't find Him no more ... the baby not the angel. Well, we cain't find *him* no more neither but he's the one what found us to begin with ... the angel ... not the baby. We done looked in every manger in town, but cain't find Him. Jest between us, I thank they moved him sommers else ... the baby ... not the angel.

But we gonna' keep our eyes open any way and see if we can spot that big old star they had on in the sky. I'm tellin' ya it were a light! It were a light fit fer a king!

Melchior,
The Man Who Saw His Star

Scripture reference-Matthew 2:7-12

I believe it was the philosopher Darius the Foolish who wrote, "As are the sands in the desert, so are the bunions on my feet." You were right, Darius, and I must soon find something upon which to sit that does not move or spit ... or I shall fall down and be buried in this desolate wasteland. This trip has been grueling. The next time Balthazar suggests a pilgrimage I think I shall have him assassinated. Perhaps I should have myself assassinated for having listened to him in the first place.

Oh my! Forgive me, I don't mean to be rude. I fear I have traveled among these uncivilized tribesmen so long I have lost my manners. My name is Melchior. I am a reader of the stars and I have come from ... well, let's just say I come from East of here. I made this pilgrimage to see the King of the Jews. Balthazar is a scholar of the Holy Scrolls. He and I believed that the Christ had recently been born and we were right. People often confuse us for one another although I can't imagine why! He is a good deal shorter than I ... and a good deal uglier, especially now whenever I try to walk. It was Balthazar who insisted we make this journey. Personally, I would have been content to simply know of His arrival from the warmth of home, but Balthazar insisted that until we saw Him, we would never be sure He was indeed the true Messiah. Caspar, who is the wealthiest of the three added that this would be a once-in-a-lifetime chance. He made all the arrangements, and we were off.

We of course went to Jerusalem. That is where one might expect to find the King of the Jews. As we began our journey, we were determined to simply follow the unusual star I had noticed wherever it would take us. However, it disappeared one night in the midst of our journey. Rather than turn back, we decided to go on ... to Jerusalem. After all, the Messiah was to be of the seed of David and Solomon. When we asked King Herod where he was entertaining the young king-to-be, the man turned absolutely crimson and began to curse and threaten his scribes. He knew nothing about the Messiah at all. His advisors found mention of a village nearby named Bethlehem in an ancient passage, but I was unsure of the purpose of their advice. I studied the sky again and there it was, the Messiah's star had reappeared. We followed the star a short distance and we found the child in ... perhaps I had best keep the location to myself, but it was a simple home like hundreds of others found in Israel.

We kept our visit short for fear we were being followed. A caravan our size is hard to hide. We gave gold to the child in honor of His kingship, Frankincense in honor of His deity and myrrh ... well, Balthazar will need to explain the myrrh. I never did follow his logic on that. We all agreed not to return to Herod or tell him where we found the Holy Child. That man has the personal charisma of a wild boar, and he rather smelled like one as well.

The only thing good about this trip has been that we did indeed get to see Him. We saw the king whose star I found in the sky nearly two years ago, the Christ, the Messiah of all Israel. Well, it's time to start walking again so long as God will heal my feet. And I do praise you Jehovah, for allowing me to see the one you have chosen to bring salvation and light to the world.

⸎

Micah,
The Man Who Made Room

Scripture reference-Luke 2:4-7

Nathan! Ezra! You boys get in here and back to work or I'm going to cut you up and feed you to the elephants! My God, what did I ever do to deserve such misfortune? Lord, when was it that you looked down on poor old Micah the Innkeeper and said, "Why look at that! Micah the Innkeeper is enjoying his life much too much! How can I destroy his happiness forever? Oh, yes, I have it! I shall send him the curse of ... children!"

Welcome to Bethlehem ... the armpit of Israel! Please forgive me, I am normally much more hospitable, but this census has come at a most unfortunate time. For the first time in two years, my inn is full, and my two lazy sons have chosen this moment to turn invisible! Once I find them, I shall sell them both to Egyptian slave traders.

For a week now, people from all over the world have come flooding into Bethlehem, each screaming at me in their own language. "Your beds are too uncomfortable!" "Excuse please, but your food tastes like slop." "You are charging me how much? For that little closet that you call a room?" "Now I don't mean to complain but from the smell of my room, something died in there ... and not too recently at that!" My wife and I are pushed to our limits taking care of thankless guests and where are my demon-seed descendants? In the kitchen, cooking or cleaning? No. In the stable, tending the animals? Of course not! At the market, running errands for their mother? No! Wake up and smell the goat's breath! Nathan! Ezra! Get back here you sons of Satan or I shall rent out your rooms! Ooh! That's not a bad idea. They can sleep with the dogs.

I promise you I am not usually so crude. I am normally a most generous and compassionate man. Why just this morning, a man from Galilee came to my door with a very young and very ill wife sitting on scraggly old donkey. He asked for a room which I could not offer him. Then I realized that his wife was in a family way and might actually deliver the child out there in the street. Well, I told him they could stay in the stable if they wanted and I led them around to the back and helped get her settled. That poor little girl. I wonder what terrible sin she committed that God would send her the curse of children at such a tender age. Oh ... she has no idea what lies ahead for her. After all her hours of labor and all her love and sacrifice, she will finally hold her newborn child in her arms ... and he will throw up all over her. Then, as the child grows older, he will find more and more creative ways to keep throwing up on her.

Ezra! Nathan! Get in here this minute. There are floors to sweep, linens to change, dishes to wash and animals to tend to! You have five minutes before I send your grandmother out to look for you! She has the nose of a bloodhound, the teeth of a lion, and the disposition of a hungry vulture. What a wonderful family I have. Oh ... the joys of fatherhood. Oh ... the curse of children!

Boy,
The Young Man Who Served Him

Original character not found in scripture

You can call me "Boy." Everybody does. My given name is Benjamin, but I like it when the shopkeepers call me Boy. I remember when I was just a little kid, Micah handed me a broom and told me to sweep in front of the Inn. He asked my name and I just blurted out, "Call me whatever you like as long as you pay me." He laughed, patted my shoulder and said, "Good boy!" I liked it. So, whenever someone yells "Hey boy! Help me unload my cart," Or "Boy, did you clean out the stall yet?" it makes me remember Micah's kindness that day. I can almost feel his hand patting my shoulder.

But you better not call my brother, Thomas, *boy*! Micah made that mistake once ... and only once. My brother bristled, stood up as tall as he could and said, "My name is Thomas, sir. I won't answer to anything else." Micah stared at him a minute then responded, "All right, Thomas. I'll remember that." Thomas is so brave, but then he's almost a man.

We never knew who our father was, Thomas and me. I don't even remember our mother or what our life had been like before she died, except for the little Thomas told me. We grew up here in Bethlehem he says, but we don't have any family left. But that's okay, we get by. Miriam lets us sleep in the stable at the Inn as long as we keep it clean and feed the animals at night. Oh, Miriam is Micah's wife; she's the closest thing to a mother I've ever known. During the day, we do odd jobs for the other local merchants. Micah is trying to help us find someone to take Thomas on as an apprentice, but times are hard now and jobs are scarce.

Thomas really likes fixing stuff but taking care of the animals is my favorite thing. Can I tell you a secret? Sometimes, the animals talk to me. Really. I look into their eyes and they tell me stuff; it's like I can read their minds, like I know what they're thinking. I'll ask about how they got this scar or why their hide is so dirty. And it's like they know what I'm saying, and I can hear them telling me their stories.

Micah says I have a real knack with animals. To him, a donkey is a donkey is a donkey, but to me they're all different. I know donkeys can be stubborn and stiff-necked but mostly they're misunderstood. Most of them are sweet and gentle. I can usually tell by their eyes if they're tired or sore or just in a bad mood. If I talk nicely to them, they'll usually nuzzle up against my shoulder while they eat, trying to get as close to me as they can, like I'm a long-lost friend. Some of them though are stiff and skittish when they arrive, like they're scared I'm going to beat them. That's probably what their masters do. I always try to sing to them while I brush their coats. Most of them like my singing ... a little too much at times. Once they join in I have to stop.

You can learn a lot though, listening to animals. They see the world through different eyes. And they all know Father God, or at least they know who He is. When I'm really scared, it helps me to talk to an animal. They always remind me that whatever happens, we have a Heavenly Father who watches out for us. I figure that if God takes care of sparrows that fall or sheep who get lost, then He's sure to take care of Thomas and me. I ask my animal friends to talk to God for me. I pray too, but I don't imagine God listens to a kid like me. Nobody else ever does. Grownups always want to tell me stuff, but they don't want to listen to me. No one ever asks me what I'm thinking or dreaming about or what I really want to be one day. Animals are good listeners ... except for cats maybe.

Something really, really cool happened one night when Thomas and I were asleep in the stable. Jesus was born right here. The animals woke me up so I wouldn't miss it. Thomas and I didn't even know they were here. There was a nice lady named Mary. Her husband, Joseph, propped her up so she could sit on the soft hay and he laid the baby in the manger which he had fixed up nice. When Mary saw me hiding in the hay, she motioned me over to her. "Do you need me to fetch anything, lady? Some water ... or something?" She smiled at me and said, "I'm fine, son. This must seem awfully frightening to someone your age. Don't be afraid. My name is Mary. What's yours?" I said that everyone just calls me Boy. Well she didn't like that.

"I mean what is your given name, son?" I didn't answer right away ... probably because she called me son. No one had ever called me that. Thomas chimed in, "His given name is Benjamin." "Then that's what I'll call you. Let me introduce you to my son, Jesus. He's a gift from God." Then, she hugged me. And she kept hugging me. I guess I had forgotten what being hugged was like ... by a human that is. And then Joseph brought the baby to her and gestured for Thomas and me to get a closer look. Joseph stood right behind me and put his hand on my shoulder just like Micah had done years before.

Joseph and Mary are kind of like family now. I really like them and sometimes Mary lets me take care of Jesus for her. It's nice not to be the little one anymore. Joseph has been teaching Thomas how to work with wood and he says his work is almost good enough for him to open his own shop soon. Mary fixed us up so we both have our own rooms ... inside the house ... with our own beds!

Miriam still feeds us at the stable, but she's making Micah pay me now for my work. The problem is that something is happening to me. Thomas says I'm just growing up but it's harder and harder to hear the animals now. They don't talk to me as much as they used to ... or maybe it's that I have people to talk to now. I just don't want anything to change any more ... ever. I have a family and a job and food to eat and hugs whenever I want one. I know they're not really my parents. After all, Thomas is only a couple of years younger than Joseph. But I hope Mary and Joseph stay here so I can teach Jesus how to hear animals talk, and about our Father in Heaven and the angels who camp around us all the time watching over and protecting us.

Joseph said that Jesus isn't really his son; he's only taking care of Him for His real Father in Heaven. I told him I know what it's like to grow up without your real father. Maybe I can help Jesus like Thomas always did for me. I don't want Him to ever feel alone. With me and the animals around, He'll never be alone.

Simeon,
The Man Who Recognized Him

Scripture reference~Luke 2:25~35

God does not lie, Simeon. God's promises are true. No matter how long you must wait, God will always keep His Word." That's what I must tell myself every morning. I must force myself out of bed by saying, "Today will be the day. Today. Today, the Messiah will appear at the Temple." I wash myself, put on clean garments and make my daily trek to the Temple Court just as I have done faithfully for years. You see, I believe the Holy Spirit of God once promised me my old eyes would see the Lord's Christ, the promised deliverer of Israel.

I sit here in the Temple court watching people as they pass by, on their way to sacrifice or do business or as they gather to gossip about the news of the day. No matter what they think, I am not senile or blind or deaf. I hear them talking about me. They don't even whisper any more. They carry on conversations in front of me as if I'm not even there. "Well, here he is again, Old Simeon the prophet. How's it going, old man?" "Why does he sit here all day every day?" "What? You don't know? Old Simeon is our Messiah watch dog, aren't you, old man? He expects to see our promised deliverer." "Well, he better come soon if Simeon is going to see him. Your hourglass is about out of sand isn't it, Simeon?"

Occasionally, someone will bring me food or try to give me money assuming I'm a well-dressed beggar. They just don't understand. God promised to send us a deliverer and He always keeps His Word. For years I have sat here in the Temple Court praying, "Lord, let the time be now. Deliver us now, oh God." Then I sit and wait for the Lord to answer, but He is silent. I have whimpered in my disappointment, "Why Lord? Why have you forsaken us?" But even in dark times of passing despair, there grows in my breast a seed of faith. "God does not lie, Simeon. God's promises are true. God will deliver us from the curse of sin and my eyes will see the long-awaited Messiah."

SIMEON, THE MAN WHO RECOGNIZED HIM

And today ... today! Today, after all these years, He is here. I have seen the Christ. After centuries of wandering through the desert of fear, staving off the sword of persecution, and the flood of loneliness ... after centuries of aimless wanderings and shattered hopes ... after centuries of bondage to sin and the tyranny of shattered dreams ... now. Now. Now, He is held before me, the Lion of Judah, the Hope of Salvation. The chosen Messiah has come to us not as a warrior or a King, but as a child. A baby who will be called Wonderful, The Mighty God, the Prince of Peace.

Yet, as I stared at the Holy Child and joy filled the emptiness of my soul, the Lord's Word spoke through me one last time. I looked into the eyes of His father as he held the baby and I took His mother's quivering hand. "Your child will be great but know this. A sword shall pierce your heart. You must not fear. God will be with you just as He has been with me. His power and strength will sustain you." Lord, now let your servant depart according to Your promise. For my eyes have seen Your salvation, which You have prepared for all people, the light of the Gentiles and the glory of Thy people Israel.

Lazarus,
The Man Who Died

Scripture reference-John 11:43-44

I don't remember much about that day. My sisters, Mary and Martha, have told the story so many times from their perspective, but I have to take their word for a lot of it. I remember being sick. It was a slow process, getting weaker every day, and sometimes I had trouble getting my breath. I told myself, "Lazarus, you are such a hypochondriac. You're not sick, you're just old! This must be what happens to a man once he gets to a certain age." I tried to tough it out, to ignore it. My sisters made that almost impossible. I know, they worry about me, but then they have always worried about me. Being an only son with two older sisters is a lot like having three mothers, one who gave me birth and two who nearly killed me.

Martha was convinced I wasn't eating enough. She fed me all kinds of exotic herbs and roots, guaranteed to fatten me up. It was succeeding, I was definitely gaining weight, but it didn't make me feel better. It's even harder to breathe with an over-stuffed belly! I was convinced I just needed to get outside more, into the fresh air. I tried my best to go for long walks every morning. One day though I nearly passed out by the road, so I started taking one of the servants with me in case I needed help getting back home. I expected that he would simply offer me a little support should I ever need it, but then during one unfortunate morning walk I ran out of breath and fainted by the road. He thought I was dead. He ran home and raised a racket and Mary came to fetch me with a cart and three burly neighbors, who were less than pleased to see me still alive. I was so mortified. As soon as we got home, Mary called for the doctor. She didn't even ask me. She knew I found him to be a most unpleasant man and would never have allowed him in my home. The two of them ganged up on me and ordered me to my bed. But after hours of having leeches suck the blood from my legs and trying to choke down his foul elixirs, Martha walked in and had a fit. She called the man a quack, said I was still as white as a sheet, and summarily threw him out. Thank you, Martha!

Finally, my sisters decided it was time to call my Galilean friend, Jesus of Nazareth. He and I had become very close over the two years I had known Him. I feel as comfortable with Him as if He were my brother. What an amazing man and a Prophet sent from Jehovah God. He could quote the Holy Scriptures word for word, but He made them sound reasonable and profound. The priests have a tendency to rattle them off without any kind of emotion or even interest. Jesus and I had often talked well into the night about our Father, Jehovah. Occasionally even Mary got involved in our discussions and Jesus spoke as freely with her as He did with me—her gender meant nothing to Him. He seemed to see inside us ... down to the very core of our souls. I have heard that God has done miracles through Him and His prayers have healed the sick and lame. There are even lepers who claim they were cleansed when they obeyed His instructions.

The girls called for Him, but all our messengers came back with no reply. That's the last I remember, lying in bed and hearing my sisters talking about how Jesus had let us down. They were afraid I might die before He could get there to heal me. That must be what happened.

The next thing I remember was hearing someone calling my name. It was pitch black, even though I was sure my eyes were open. "Lazarus!" It was a familiar voice and I tried to respond but couldn't. Again, the voice called for me, a little louder than before. "Lazarus!" I shook my head and a cloth fell from my face. I began to come to my senses as if I were waking from a deep sleep. "Lazarus!" I felt like my bed clothes had been twisted in the night and I struggled to sit up. I became aware that I was not in my room as I had thought but on a slab of rock in a cold cave. I saw a beam of light at one end of the cave, so I tried to rise and move toward it. "Lazarus!" I tried to answer but my throat was too dry even to speak. I was struggling with the strips of cloth wrapped tightly around my body, trying to free my legs and arms.

"Lazarus, come forth!" I dragged my feet out into the daylight and suddenly the voice stopped. I thought I must have gone deaf because I heard absolutely nothing, not a gust of wind or a bird's call ... nothing. "The man needs help getting free of his graveclothes!" I finally recognized the voice; it was Jesus who had called me from my grave. Suddenly, I was surrounded by people ... Mary and Martha kissing me, and a hundred hands pulled at my bandages. They told me I had died ... but Jesus had raised me from the dead.

The next day is a blur. I remember being hungry and so very, very thirsty! Jesus stayed with us for much too short a time and then both sisters tried to tell me what had happened. They were both speaking at the same time though, so it took me a while to sort it all out. Plus, they began to argue over who did what and who said what first. I finally knew I was well again, when I yelled at them ... full voice as if I were twenty years old again. "Mary, Martha, I love you both, but can you stop arguing for just a few moments." All of us burst into laughter and fell into a group hug while tears flowed freely down our cheeks. "It's a miracle!" Martha said. I must agree. It was a miracle indeed!

Orem,
The Man Who Welcomed Him

Scripture reference~Matthew 21:8~15
(Video available)

"Hosanna! Help us! Blessed is He who comes in the name of ... oh, it's only Nabob the beggar! Save it! It's not him."

Oh, shalom, are you here for the demonstration? Just grab a palm branch and ... what? What demonstration? What are you, from out of town? Everyone in Jerusalem is talking about it. We're here to welcome this new prophet from Galilee who is supposed to arrive sometime today ... although punctual He's not! Apparently, He's some sort of a Miracle Man, who has healed people of all kinds of diseases. Tamar, that's my second cousin on my mother's stepfather's side of the family, she said she watched Him heal a boy who was blind from birth. And Doofus, who is my sister's second husband's father, said he watched Him walk on water. Although Doofus may not be the most reliable witness in the world ... he drinks like a fish. But other more reliable witnesses say this man may be the Messiah. Excuse me for one moment would you please? Talk amongst yourselves. "Jeroboam! *(as if to a fellow palm waver)* Keep your eyes on the horizon. You are looking for a thirty-something Jewish male, not a twenty-something female!"

What? Well, yes of course I realize we've had many Messiahs before and not much ever came of it. But this one sounds different. All of the others built their reputations by killing people. They all went off in the desert, built up an army then raided Roman supply caravans. But this Jesus, that's the man's name, the Miracle Man, He talks a lot about love and forgiveness. And He must be one really really nice guy because little kids will run and jump up on His lap like He's an old friend of the family. And Malchus, a friend of my third cousin twice removed, the cousin not the friend, he says that according to the holy scrolls the true Messiah will come with miracles, signs, and wonders to prove that He is indeed the Messiah, the Son of the

OREM, THE MAN WHO WELCOMED HIM

Living God. After all, you gotta like a man who turns water into wine, don't you?

Oh! Here He is! "Hosanna! Help us! Blessed is He who ... false alarm! It's not Him. It's just Arphaxad the cloth merchant ... you blind son of a cross-eyed Philistine. You're looking for a man in his thirties. That old pirate has got to be at least ... a hundred!"

What? Why am I here? Oh ... you mean why am I here? Why am I here? Why am I here? That's a very good question. Why am I here? I hadn't thought. You must be smarter than you look. I don't know. I guess I need to see him for myself. I've been praying for years that the real Messiah would come and give those Roman bloodsuckers what they deserve. Why do I hate the Romans? Wow! You *must* be from out of town. There's almost no one left in Jerusalem who hasn't lost someone to Roman arrogance. For your information I once watched my own mother run over by a Roman chariot. Then the magistrate had my father flogged because the accident hurt one of his horses. My mother was laying in the middle of the road bleeding, but all the man cared about was his stinking animals. Well, one day the Lion of Judah will rise up and feast on Roman flesh!

What? Are you sure? Oh ... he's riding a donkey. It must be Him. "Hosanna! Help us! Blessed is He who ... Wrong again! It's not Him. It's just Fat Fatima the pig herder's wife." Well I can't get upset with Jeroboam over that one. It was an honest mistake. Please! That woman's hips are so wide that when she waddles down the road it looks like she's hiding a donkey under her tunic! I just hope this Jesus is for real. I'm so tired of getting my hopes up just to have them run over by Roman chariots. One day the real Messiah will come, and all Israel will be able to stand up and say with a single voice, "No! No, Caesar, all the raping and pillaging will have to stop now! No, Caesar, we're not going to pay your exorbitant taxes anymore! No, Caesar, you will not treat us worse than animals!"

What? Are you sure? Is he riding a donkey? Okay, can you actually see a donkey? You can? Does it look like He's in His thirties? It does? Is He surrounded by Galileans, you know fisherman types and such? He is? Then it must be Him. He's finally here. Please, Jehovah, let this one be the right one. Please. I'm not sure how much longer I can keep hope alive. "Hosanna! Help us! Blessed is He who comes in the name of the Lord!"

Seth,
The Man Who Watched Him Die

Scripture reference-Matthew 27:48-50

Most young men want to be rich when they grow up. Some dare to dream of becoming a warrior or an athlete. Others, from the time they are very young, seem to have their hearts set on raising a family, a large family with four or five wives. But as for me, I have always wanted to help dying people. Yes, you heard me correctly. Let me explain. If a man is very sick and the family cannot ... or will not care for him, they call for me. I sit with those who are beyond medical help. I hold their hand, so they won't feel alone or deserted as they pass. Sometimes I sing to them or quote King David's psalms. Then, when their spirit has finally left the body, I close their eyes, wash their faces and wounds, straighten their hair, dress them nicely and call for the family and the mourners.

I also give drugged wine to condemned criminals at public executions. For crucifixions, I hoist it up in a sop tied to a spear. It doesn't stop their pain, but it reduces it somewhat. In my lifetime I have witnessed seven hundred forty-three passings ... more than half of which occurred at the hands of the Romans. The Soldiers just call me "the Wine Giver." I consider that a compliment.

It's not that I enjoy watching people die. I have simply never felt the need to fear it. Somehow, I cannot see death as an ending, but as a kind of second birth. A child doesn't ask to be born yet it happens, nonetheless. I've never met a sane person who wanted to die either, but neither process can be avoided, only postponed. You cannot stop a baby from leaving the womb and you cannot keep a man from dying. But just as a mother holds her newborn and helps him make a more gentle and calm entrance into our world, I try to offer the same kindness as they leave us. I stay close by and try to comfort them as they pass into a new life ... gently and with dignity.

I take pride in my work. After all these years one would expect me to be able to do my job as if it were any other everyday task, like making a fire or sweeping the floor. But every time I watch someone pass from this world ... yes, each and every time I am filled with wonder. I ask myself the same questions over and over again. How does this happen? Where do they go? Are they at peace in their new world, or in hellish torment? Do they simply fall asleep or do they remember what happened to them here? One might think I would have answers for these questions by now, but I am more convinced than ever that there are no answers to be found ... at least not among the living.

Today, I watched a Galilean die on a cross. The Romans say He was a heretic; that He claimed to be the only son of Jehovah. A number of unsavory men circulated through the crowd paying people to curse Him. But, at His feet there were several women weeping uncontrollably, insisting on His innocence and begging the soldiers to spare His life. Two other criminals hung on crosses on either side of Him. At first, they bit their lips and sneered at the crowd. They were fighting the pain, trying to ignore it. That first phase normally lasts about two or three hours. Then come pleas for mercy, then curses, and finally defeat and surrender. I watch the prisoners' faces closely to see when the wine will do the most good. If given too early, it can weaken their resolve to breathe, but if I wait too long, the pain is too intense for the wine to offer any comfort. The man on the center cross, the Galilean, kept searching the sky. Only occasionally would He look down at me, but when He did, I saw something in His eyes that I had never seen before in the eyes of a condemned man ... compassion. He seemed more concerned about my pain than His own. It was as if He was asking me, "Are you all right? I'm so sorry you have to see this."

Toward the end, I heard Him say to one of the other men, "Today you will join me in paradise." Paradise. What a beautiful thought. I can't get that picture out of my mind. Paradise! In my mind's eye I can see the Galilean putting his arm around his co-sufferer and leading him through Heavenly gates into a glorious city, whose builder and maker is God. If only there is such a place, a paradise where people go when their earthly lives are over. I think it may be true. I do! I believe it must be true. Thank you, Galilean. From this day forward, I will carry that picture in my mind ... and written on my heart. Perhaps one day I too will join You ... in Paradise.

Judas Iscariot,
The Man Who Betrayed Him

Scripture reference-Matthew 26:14-16

I've never met a man like Jesus. He's a nobody, like me, but He doesn't seem to realize it. Personally, I can't see why everybody likes Him so much. He is kinda' handsome, I suppose, but a lot of the time He talks in riddles, like He's so much smarter than anyone else. How smart could He be? After all, He was born and raised in Nazareth, the armpit of Israel, and people who know the family, say Jesus' mother wasn't even married when she gave birth to Him. Yet He acts like … I don't know, like He walks on water.

When He and His buddies came by and invited me to travel with them, I thought they were offering me a job.

"Well, how much does it pay?"

"Nothing."

"Where do we live? I mean, do you have a home base?"

"No, we sleep wherever we end up and eat whatever my Heavenly Father provides."

"What? You don't have a budget, or working capital?"

"No, Judas, I offer you a life filled with sacrifice and hardship—and spiritual riches beyond your wildest imagination."

I thought He was joking, you know, leading me on, trying to make the ignorant country boy look stupid, but He was serious. I looked around at His disciples. There were a few fishermen, a couple of working stiffs, and one crazy man. They called him Simon, "Simon the zealot." "Simon the freak" would have been more like it. He had hair like dry seaweed and dark eyes that bugged out like he was about to explode. However, Jesus also had a wealthy tax collector with Him, and a couple of guys who dressed like they had some serious

JUDAS ISCARIOT, THE MAN WHO BETRAYED HIM

money. I thought to myself, "If rich men follow Jesus, they must see a chance for some kind of profit. And face it, Judas, you're never going to get ahead in this hick town. This may be your only shot at the big time." So, I went with them.

He herded us all over Israel. Every weirdo, leper, and crackpot in Galilee ran after us, begging Jesus to heal them. It was pathetic. But instead of saying, "Get away from me you sickos," He told them to believe in His Heavenly Father, and they would be all fixed up. To one guy He had the nerve to say, "Your sins are forgiven." I thought, "Oh man, He's lost it. He's gone too far this time. The priests have killed men for a lot less."

Finally, we ended up in Jerusalem, and all of a sudden, Jesus went nuts. He threw over the money-changers' tables in the Temple and sent several of them rolling down the steps on their ears. Those merchants have been there for generations. People depend on them. Jesus was acting like a madman. And from the moment we hit Jerusalem, a mob of seedy-looking men followed us around, probably friends of Crazy Simon. They were talking rebellion, you know, war against the Romans. Jesus sorta blew them off, thank God, but it worried me. What would happen if Jesus suddenly said, "Okay guys, time to overthrow the government!" I had to do something to keep Him from getting us all killed.

I went to talk to Caiaphas, just to talk. He's a reasonable man. I told him I was a friend of Jesus, but I was worried about Him. Caiaphas said he was worried about him too. We decided it would be best if we locked Him up for a while, for His own good. Somebody had to protect Him from the revolutionaries. Annas said that they would use Romans, like He was being arrested, just to make things look official. So, I took the soldiers to find Jesus. As we entered the Garden of Gethsemane, I pushed through the crowd, like I didn't know what was going on, and kissed Jesus. That was the signal.

Hey, don't act so high and mighty. I was the only one of the twelve who had the guts to do something to keep Jesus from hurting Himself and all of Israel with Him. The priests just want to scare Him back to His senses and let things settle down a little. I have Caiaphas' promise that they won't hurt Him. They're going to hold Him in protective custody a little while ... just a day or two at most. That's all.

When Jesus gets out of prison, I'll give Him the thirty pieces of silver the priests gave me for my help. Hey, I didn't ask for it, they just gave it to me.

JUDAS ISCARIOT, THE MAN WHO BETRAYED HIM

He'll understand why I did ... what I did. You'll see! A couple of days from now, everyone will thank me. A couple of days from now, I'll be a hero. Yeah. Just a day ... or two.

Simon Peter,
The Man Who Repented

Scripture reference-John 18:25-27
(Video available)

When I first met Jesus, I was mending nets with my brother Andrew. Our father was melting tar to fix a small crack in the side of our boat, and as usual, complaining. "Why I remember a time when a man could throw out his net in the morning and by evening it would take forty men to haul in the catch. Oh well, can't get good help nowadays no-how." Papa talked like that every time he had to work with hot tar.

We were just about to break for lunch, when this wild-eyed Galilean walked over to us and said, "Leave your nets and come with me. I'll teach you to be fishers of men." Andrew looked at me ... I looked back at him, and without a word, we did it.

We dropped our nets and just walked off with that man. To this day I don't know why. There was just something about Him, a certain presence ... I don't know, the way He spoke with authority, the way He looked directly into a person's soul, the way He walked ... like the whole Earth belonged to Him. It was as if I had known Him for years, and that somehow, He knew me.

For the next three years, we wandered throughout Israel, watching Him heal the sick and deliver people from all kinds of bondages. I suppose Jesus knew where we were going and why, but if He did, He never felt the need to share His agenda with us. He just said, "Trust me. My Father in heaven will take care of us." He was right. Jesus became our rabbi, our mentor ... our friend.

By the time we reached Jerusalem, people were calling Jesus "The Miracle Man." He hated that! A huge crowd ran out to meet us. They paved the way with palm branches and shouted, "Hosanna, deliver us!" as if we were conquerors. I'd never seen a demonstration like that before, for anyone. But Jesus wasn't impressed by the crowds or their cries of loyalty. He seemed troubled ... not like He was worried, just ... troubled, like a man who is about to sail off into unfamiliar waters. As we sat in the

SIMON PETER, THE MAN WHO REPENTED

upper room to celebrate the Passover meal with Him, Jesus was downright sad. It wasn't like Him. I told a couple of jokes to kinda lighten the mood and He laughed ... politely. His heart wasn't in it though. To look at Him, you'd think the world was about to end. It was.

That very night, I stood on the hill of Golgotha, and watched Roman soldiers attach my friend to a rough-hewn wooden cross. It all happened so fast. One minute, we were praying in Gethsemane, and the next, Jesus had been arrested, beaten within an inch of His life, and was being tried for heresy. I found myself huddled by a fire, trying to get a glimpse of Jesus to find out what they had done to Him, scared to death that someone would recognize me as one of His followers and beat me as well. A little girl noticed I was Galilean and simply asked if I had ever met Jesus ... and I freaked out. I cursed at that little girl and said, "I never knew Him." As soon as the words had left my lips, I looked up and Jesus stopped as the soldiers led Him away. He looked me straight in the eyes and somewhere ... in the distance ... I heard a rooster crow. All my plans, my hopes, even my self-respect died that night ... nailed to a rough-hewn wooden cross.

It's been two days now since Jesus ... since He was ... I came back here, to this upper room where we ate together. I cannot force myself to leave Jerusalem ... not yet. I feel the need to be with people that knew Him the way I knew Him, people who believed in Him the way I believed in Him, people that loved Him the way I ... Tomorrow morning, a few of the women are going with Jesus' mother to anoint the body with spices. It's strange, I can still feel His presence here, as if He's still sitting right there.

"Jesus, how could you do it? How could you sit there and look at us and smile at us and eat with us and even laugh at my stupid jokes when all along you knew what I was about to ... Jesus, I hope you know how much I loved you. I hope you can find a way to forgive my cowardice. Then maybe you can teach me how to forgive myself."

Octavian,
The Man Who Guarded the Tomb

Scripture reference~Matthew 28:11~15

I am not a coward, sir! Nor am I an idiot who could be hoodwinked by a bunch of overly zealous fishermen! I'm telling you there was nothing for us to fight! Look, sir, you obviously don't believe me so let me start again at the beginning. Try to listen to what I'm telling you, sir, not what you expect me to say. Please sir! We did nothing wrong.

I am a faithful servant to Rome. I worship Caesar and the gods. I have served here in Judea for five years now and I am well familiar with religious fanatics. I know their tricks, and I know every hiding place in Jerusalem. If I hadn't seen this with my own eyes, I would be every bit as skeptical as you are. Ask Flavius! He chose me for this detail because I am not a man who can be easily deceived.

My unit was chosen to guard the Galilean's tomb. I thought we were being punished for something because it is not our usual procedure to guard the graves of crucified criminals. As a matter of fact, their carcasses are usually left on the crosses as long as possible as a warning to other rebel groups. A lot of times they rot and fall off by themselves; there is so little left of them once the birds and jackals have eaten their fill. Apparently though a wealthy Jew bribed Pilate to surrender the body of the Galilean and lay it in a new tomb nearby, so we had to hoist Him down off the cross, so they could wrap his body for burial.

Flavius himself came with us to the garden and he made sure that none of the man's disciples would be able to abscond with his remains and start some new freaky religion with them. After he was sure there were no other caverns connected to the cave, we rolled a huge stone in front of the entrance. It took five men to roll it into place and believe me it was not going anywhere any time soon! But as if that wasn't enough, Flavius had us secure the stone with braces and ropes and put Caesar's stamp on it. If anyone messed with it, there would be clear evidence of tampering. Then he commanded me and my men to remain on watch to ward off grave robbers. "Seriously? We're defending graves now?"

We set up camp in the garden, right in front of the tomb. It was a pretty boring detail. I had to watch carefully to make sure none of the men drank too much or wandered off. I tried to impress on them the value of our mission, sir. "Our duty here is just as important as if we were in battle or guarding the governor himself." I felt a little foolish trying to convince them of something I didn't believe myself, but I said it nonetheless, sir.

But just before dawn, there was an earthquake. Surely you felt it! It tossed us around like we were nothing. There was a flash of lightning and then it was over. A couple of my men checked to see if anyone was hurt, but I ran to the tomb. The stone hadn't been rolled away, sir—it had been pushed over ... from the inside. And the body was just gone. Yes sir, I realize the penalty for lying to an officer! There had not been a soul in that Garden that night, but the body had just vanished. Yes, I was asleep until the earthquake but there were two sentries, two of my best men, who swear that the grave had exploded turning that huge boulder into gravel. The lightning must have hit it.

My men and I were afraid to report this, sir. We even talked about running away or taking our own lives. We knew you would assume we had been derelict in our duties. But sir, what did we do wrong? What did we NOT do that we should have done to prevent this? We are trained soldiers but none of us were trained to do battle against an earthquake.

Thank you, sir. I'm glad you finally believe me. I'm sorry, sir, could you say that again? I must instruct my men to say that the Galilean's disciples had overpowered us and stolen the body? But sir, we will be branded as cowards ... Yes sir, I am grateful to be alive and yes, I wish to stay that way. Thank you, sir. My men will say whatever ... you're also going to pay us for our trouble? So ... you're paying us to take responsibility for the loss of Jesus' body? But you do promise that none of us will be court-martialed, am I correct? Then so be it. His body was stolen. Thank you again, sir. Hail Caesar!

Thomas,
The Man Who Doubted

Scripture reference-John 20:26-29

I have never been especially fond of people. I choose to live free of personal entanglements, the unreasonable demands lovers lavish on those they claim to care about. People throw the word "love" around as if it were as common and cheap as sand. "I love God." "I love my priest." "I love my new home." "I love my sheep." How often I have heard men justify the most abominable treatment of their wives or children with a simple, "I'm only doing this because I love you." I suspect most of them are lying through their teeth and totally incapable of loving anything but themselves. If people truly understood the meaning of the word and the kind of selfless commitment it demands, we would never hear it used again.

It was difficult for me to accept the teachings of Jesus. I wanted desperately to believe in Him, but his words seemed a little too good to be true. In my lifetime, I have known precious few people who proved themselves worthy of my love and trust, including the priests. I decided to follow Jesus to see for myself if He truly was a prophet sent from God, or merely another charlatan spouting pious words to deceive the feeble-minded. Far too many people believe that in order to prove your loyalty to a leader, you must blind yourself to their flaws. According to them, one must accept every platitude with the same naive stupidity of a little boy who actually believes that the beating that just left him bruised and bleeding, actually hurt his father more than it hurt him. That is not devotion; that is ignorance. In order to love someone, you must know them completely. You must love their flaws as well as their strengths, but you cannot ... no, you dare not ignore them. Love does not turn its face from a multitude of sins; it covers them with a blanket of forgiveness.

I loved and trusted Jesus, in my own way, but I also scrutinized His every word. First, I wanted to be sure I understood what He was teaching, but second, I wanted to prevent the Pharisees from twisting His words to discredit Him. Some of the others resented me for it. "You must not question the master," they would say. But Jesus understood. I think He came to appreciate the fact that I would not allow Him to wander off into heresy or slide unaware into the pit of hypocrisy. Jesus knew that my questions were not offered out of disagreement, but out of love. After Jesus was ... taken from us, I distanced myself from the others. Andrew insisted we stay in Jerusalem, at least for a few days, and I agreed, but I thought, "What's the point? Jesus was the bond that united us all. Without Him ... well, it's time we faced the facts. He's gone. It's over. And we were wrong. We might as well go back to our homes and get on with our lives."

Several days later, Andrew found me in the marketplace and said, "Thomas, quickly! You must come back to the upper room. There are eye-witnesses claiming that Jesus is alive again."

"Calm down," I responded, "Who started this rumor?"

"Mary Magdalene ... but it's not a rumor, Thomas. She saw Him. He even spoke to her. But that's not all. Peter and James went back to the tomb and they saw angels who confirmed that Jesus has been resurrected. Don't you understand, Thomas? The Master lives!"

"Calm down. You know, this could be some kind of trick ... staged by the Pharisees to make us look foolish ... or to flush us all out in the open."

"But what if it is true, Thomas? It would be the greatest miracle of all time."

Andrew had a very good point, so I went back to the upper room and listened to Peter and James recount the story. Simon called me a doubter. "Look, I'm only verbalizing the questions all of you should be asking yourselves. It cannot have been Jesus. There must be some other explanation for what you ..." Before I could finish my sentence, a man appeared in the middle of the room. He came out of nowhere. And He looked like ... "No," I told myself, "This is crazy." I rubbed my eyes in disbelief. "Now Thomas, get a grip. Your grief is affecting your eyesight. It's just a hallucination." But when I opened my eyes again, Jesus was still standing there, laughing at me gently and holding out His hands. The nail-scars were unmistakable.

"It's all right, Thomas. You can touch me ... if you want to ... if you need to. One day you will be able to believe without seeing, but for now, here ...

THOMAS, THE MAN WHO DOUBTED

touch my wounds. Or would you rather put your hand in my side where the spear pierced it."

Instead, I fell to my knees and wept. "My God ... you're my Lord and my God!"

✦

Mahalaleel,
The Man Who Told People

Original character not found in scripture

Have you heard the news? It's absolutely unbelievable! Well, I suppose it's not completely unbelievable, after all it really happened! So it is believable ... I mean you should believe it because it's true. Only no one's going to believe it because it is so ... unbelievable!

Hi, my name is Mahalaleel, son of Mary. No, not Mary the Mother of Jesus! Do I look like a Messiah's brother? I know her, Mother Mary that is. Actually, Mary is a very popular name right now, they're all over Jerusalem. Besides Mother Mary, there's Mary from Magdala, who comes from ... Magdala. And Fat Mary, only better not call her that to her face. And there's Tall Mary who raises the roof when she's mad at her husband. And Big Mary who keeps rollin' down the river. Like I said, there are a lot of Marys. So, everyone calls me Mahalaleel of Mary-Not-the-Mother!

That name bothered me at first ... Mahalaleel of Mary-NOT-the-Mother ... but then I realized they might have chosen something really bad ... like calling me by my father's name, Mephibosheth! Mahalaleel of Mephibosheth! Wow, that's a mouthful.

Come to think of it, why do some men have extra names? I mean Father is just "Mephibosheth" and Andrew is just "Andrew" and Peter is just "Peter," ... although I did hear one of his fishing buddies call him "Old Fishbreath" once. But why isn't John called "John of Zebedee"? Or James called "James of Alphaeus"? Or Thaddeus called Thaddeus of ... okay I have no idea where he came from.

Whoops! How did I get started talking about names? I'm sorry, I get easily distracted. I start off talking about one thing and then I realize I've drifted off again. Like right now. What were we ... Oh, that's right! I was about to tell you my unbelievable news! I mean my not so unbelievable news. Wait a minute. On second thought, maybe I shouldn't tell you. What if you don't believe me?

MAHALALEEL, THE MAN WHO TOLD PEOPLE

Nobody ever believes me when I tell them good news!

I told Rebecca about the wedding in Cana, you know, how Jesus turned the water into wine, but did she believe me? Nooo! Then she hears it from Zadok and suddenly she throws her hands in the air and praises God.

And the day Jesus multiplied the loaves and fishes, I came running home to tell my mama, Mary-Not-the-Mother, but would she believe me? Nooo! Then Andrew tells her the same thing and she's all, "Praise the Lord! How wonderful!"

And when I ran to tell Caiaphas the High Priest about how the crowd was welcoming Jesus into Jerusalem shouting, "Blessed is He who comes in the name of the Lord," he actually yelled at me and threw me out of the room. Can you believe it?

Okay, it happened again. I got distracted and I haven't told you my news yet! It's unbelievable! But you had better believe me! This morning, my mother Mary-Not-The-Mother went with some of the other Marys to the tomb where they buried Jesus. Joseph of Arimathea donated it. Oh, how about that! Joseph of Arimathea ... there's another man with extra names. And Simon of Cyrene and John the Baptist! And here I am talking about names again! And just when I was getting to the good part.

Okay I'm just going to spit it right out, but you better believe me. You promise you'll believe me? Nod your heads and say, "Yes, Mahaleel of Mary-not-the-Mother! We'll believe you!" Okay that was just sad ... but I'm going to tell you anyway!

When we got to Jesus' tomb, what do you think we found? Go ahead, guess! You'll never ... what? That's right the tomb was empty. How did you know that? And we saw two ... that's amazing! Yes, they were angels. You must be clairvoyant! And guess what they told us ... that's right! Jesus is alive again!!! God raised Him from the dead! What's wrong with you people? Jesus is alive again! Okay you promised you'd get excited! You bunch of deadheads!

Oh, I know who'll get excited for me! Blind Balthazar! Last time I told him some good news he jumped up and down like a madman for over an hour. Of course, the "good news" was that I had just found my pet snake crawling up his leg! Oh, look there he is! "Hey Balthazar, do you want to hear something unbelievable?" Boy! For a blind man he can run pretty fast.

Zacchaeus,
The Man Who Climbed a Tree

Scripture reference - Luke 19:1-10

It was seven days ago when I first learned that Jesus had entered Jericho. So, I made off to see the man. But being shorter than most ... *(If performed by a tall man- "You should see the others!")* ... and not accustomed to having favors shown me, I could not get near. So, I tried another plan. I ran on ahead and clambered onto the bough of a tree. *(If performed by a large man- "It was a very large tree.")* I waited there, sure of a good view.

   I watched Him as He drew near and thought to see Him pass and leave me behind. Instead He stopped, looked me right in the eyes and chuckled, "Zaccheaus? Zachaeus, come down. You must give me a home today."

His words quivered all through me. Is it nothing after so long a time to be treated like a man? He gave me His friendship. We outcasts must make friends with outcasts; we have no others. But what need had He of me? I clambered down as quickly as I could, bowed, and turned to lead the way to my home.

But suddenly I realized that the "weather" had changed. The light had gone out of men's faces and I saw around me nothing but anger—and contempt. Yes, I've seen all that many times before—and I gave it back to them. But was I to drag Him into the mud I was in myself? It was as if He had lost all His friends and He lost them all ... for me. Then the voices started, "Going there to eat??" "Oh yes, He'll eat from Roman plates and drink from Roman goblets ... the blood of honest Jewish merchants!" He heard it too—as well as I.

If I could have just turned on them and said, "These men slander me. Publican as I am—my hands are clean." But I could not say so. This time they were right that my home was no place for Him. Then I looked at Him ... and my eyes were opened. Beside Him we are all unworthy ... and unclean.

"Listen," I cried, "I'll give half of all I own to the poor and if I've defrauded any man of anything,

ZACCHAEUS, THE MAN WHO CLIMBED A TREE

I'll—I'll pay him back ... fourfold!" Then my tongue failed me, and I looked to Him to see if He could help me out. I could not read His thoughts but there was a smile on His face—and I became content.

Then He said, "Salvation has entered this house today. Zacchaeus too is a son of Abraham."

Those were His very words. He called me a "Son of Abraham." The Son of Man came to seek and to save that which was lost. Strange, I didn't know I was lost ... until I was found.

John,
The Man Who Outlived Them All

Scripture reference–John 21:20-25

Intently writing) "In the beginning was the logos, and the logos was with God, and the logos was God." Yes, that's good; that says it very nicely. "And the logos lived among us …" Oh, I'm sorry I didn't notice you there. When did you come in? Forgive me please, I'm trying to write a book about Jesus' life and ministry. I need to record this moment quickly, while the people who can confirm it are still alive. I get so caught up in my writing that I often forget where I am. I wish I were more like my brother, James. He always connected with people so much better than I. He said I loved words more than I loved people. I suspect he was right. I really miss him.

KEN LEE—VOICES FROM THE BIBLE

Allow me to introduce myself. My name is John, the son of Zebedee. I was one of the twelve specially chosen to walk with Jesus, the Messiah. I was privileged to study at the feet of the greatest rabbi of all time, the light of the world, the logos himself. Jesus was with Jehovah from the creation of the world, but He lived among us for a mere thirty-three years. For three of those years, I watched Him preach and teach, heal and perform miracles, eat and sleep, laugh and weep, calling Jews throughout Galilee and Judea to repent and turn to the God of Abraham. He was killed on a Roman cross but rose to new life three days later and He is now seated at the right hand of Jehovah God making intercession for all of us who trust in Him.

On the night Jesus was betrayed, he gathered the twelve of us together in an upper room in Jerusalem. It seemed like just another Passover celebration, but I couldn't help but wonder why Jesus insisted we spend it together rather than with our families. As I entered that room, there was something in the air. I can't describe it exactly, a tension, a sense of danger mixed with excitement, like the feeling in the pit of your stomach just before you dive off a cliff into a lake. Jesus was unusually quiet. We ate in silence, except for Peter, who tried to lighten the mood by telling stories that I can only assume were meant to be funny. Only two people understood the significance of that supper. Only two knew what was really happening. Only two people could see the coming storm ... only two ... the one who was to die, and the one who betrayed Him.

That very night, as we prayed in the Garden of Gethsemane, Roman soldiers came to arrest Jesus. Of course, they didn't know which of us was the real Messiah until Judas stepped from among the soldiers and shouted, "Rabbi, how are you?" Then, he kissed Jesus. It must have been some prearranged signal because the soldiers immediately pounced on the Master and took Him away. Judas, how could you have allowed yourself to become so blinded by greed? Jesus was never more than a meal-ticket to you, was he? You were so hungry for gold that you missed the greatest treasure of all ... Jesus himself.

We still gather together, the nine of us who remain, to break bread and share a cup, just as we did that night in the upper room with Jesus. James, my brother, was the first to be martyred for the sake of Jesus' gospel. And this week, we received word that Peter has been killed. He was crucified up-side down, because He didn't feel worthy to be killed in the same manner as our Lord. Good for you, Peter ... the rest of us will follow soon enough.

The Jewish leaders believe that if they kill all nine of us, that Jesus' influence will end. They are wrong. For Jesus' death on Calvary has changed forever man's relationship with Jehovah. He is the Lamb of God who has taken away the sins of the world.

I realize my life is in danger, but I also know this. God's message must go forth, and it will indeed be spread throughout the world with or without my help. Though men slay me, Jesus' words will endure. Though nations raise up armies to annihilate us, from the dust stained with our blood, God will raise up thousands and ten-thousands of witnesses who will continue to shout, "Jesus is Lord! Yes, Jesus is Lord!"

Zorak,
The Man Who Warned Pilate

Original character not found in scripture

Can you feel it? Of course, you can feel it! Do you hear it? Of course, you can hear it! Listen with the ears of your soul. See with the eyes of your spirit guide. It is the heartbeat of the universe ... boom boom ... transcending ... boom boom ... Yommmmmm. Don't just sit there, chant with me! Yommmmm. You're not chanting with me! You will never be onnnnnne with the spirit realmmmmm until you hummmmmm the proper tonnnnnnne. I can see you know nothing of religion. You are as blind as my master, Pilate.

Wait a minute! I'm getting a message from the spirits. Shhhh! I'm trying to become one with the spirit realm, but its voice is so soft. The spirits must have a touch of laryngitis! *(Selecting a member of the audience)* You madame! The spirits have told me that you were once frightened by a ... by a ... a ... fire breathing dragon when you were only ten years old. Am I right? No? Are you sure? Oh, I see more clearly now. It was not a dragon ... but an elephant who threw water at you when you were only six years old. Am I right? No? Hmmmm, now I see it clearly. You were nursed by a gorilla when you were only two years old. No? You were a baby! How would you know?

Never mind. I will sacrifice a rat to the gods for you and ask them to repair your memory. Do you have some incense on you? I go through a lot of it lately. Why? Did you just ask me why? I'll tell you why I sacrifice. Jupiter is red, Saturn refuses to enter his house, and the moon is singing to the deafened sun, that's why! We are in the middle of a crisis people. Wake up and smell the hibiscus! Pagans. I'm talking to pagans. The rhythm of the universe has been interrupted by this Galilean prisoner they call Jesus. The world is screeching to a halt. I can feel it in my bones ... no ... deeper than that ... I can feel it in my soul ... no ... deeper than that. I can feel it in my belly, my intestines, my spleen ... oh I'm making myself sick.

ZORAK, THE MAN WHO WARNED PILATE

This Jesus must be a powerful wizard, the most powerful wizard of all time! I told Mistress Claudia, Pilate's wife, "Mistress," I said, I said, "Mistress," I said ... "Mistress," I said. All right I forgot what I said. But I told her to warn Master Pilate. He must have nothing to do with this just man! Oh, I have suffered much because of Him. He walks through my dreams. First, He walked through my mind carrying a sword. Then He walked through my soul carrying a chicken. Then a fig cake. And a then a birthday cake and then ice cream and then I realized that I wasn't asleep at all. I was just hungry ... so I got up and ate a sandwich.

But that first part was right. Better leave that water walker alone! Master Pilate! All nature cries out against the death of an innocent man! You must wash your hands of him. Wash, Pilate, wash! Wash your hands of His innocent blood! Wash, Pilate, wash. You better wash them again for I can still see His blood! Seriously ... right around the fingernails. There! I think you got it! Wash, Pilate, wash.

Wait, I'm getting another message from the spirits! There is a man here ... a very handsome man ... Oh spirits are you sure you have the right room? Oh, you sir! *(selects a man in the room)* It must be you of whom the spirits speak ... because all the other men are sooooo ugly! The spirits tell me that you have a mole on the little toe of your left foot! Am I right? No? Sure, you do. Take off your shoe so I can see if you're lying. No, on second thought I don't have enough incense left for you to remove your shoe. And this room isn't well ventilated. Wait, the spirits now tell me you have a pimple on your knee. The spirits better make up their minds! Am I right? Do you have a pimple? No? Oh good, they can be really annoying! No, I have it now. You once had a pimple on your face, didn't you? Am I right? No? Don't give me that! You did so! Next time, spirits, choose a man who is more honest.

But back to the story! I must consult with the wizards and seers of Turin, and the oracle of Delphi, to see if their power can stop this Galilean from turning the world on its ear! I fear that no earthly force can stop what Jesus has begun! The life force of our world has changed forever. Oh Mars! Oh Milky Way! Oh Snickers! *O-kay* that's it, I'm obviously too hungry to prophecy. You'll have to catch me again after lunch.

Single-Character Plays for Women

Miriam,
The Innkeeper's Wife

Scripture reference-Luke 2:4-7

Nathan! Ezra! You boys get back to work or I'm going to feed you to the elephants! And find your no-account father while you're at it!

My Lord, what did I ever do to deserve such misfortune? When was it that Jehovah looked down on poor old Miriam and said, "Why look at that! Miriam is enjoying her life much too much! What can I do to destroy her happiness forever? Oh, yes, I have it! I shall send her the curse ... the curse of children!"

Welcome to Bethlehem ... the armpit of Israel! Please forgive me, I am normally much more hospitable, but this census has come at a most unfortunate time and I'm at the end of my rope. My lazy, no-good husband and I run this Inn and for the first time in two years, every room is full! So, of course my two lazy sons have chosen this moment to turn invisible! Once I find them, I think I'll sell them both to Egyptian slave traders.

For a week now, people from all over the world have come flooding into Bethlehem, each screaming at me in their own language. "Your beds are too uncomfortable!" "Excuse please, but your food tastes like slop." "You are charging me how much? For that little closet that you call a room?" "Now I don't mean to complain but from the smell of my room, something died in there ... and not too recently at that!"

My husband and I have been pushed to our limits taking care of thankless guests and constant complaints and where are my demon-seed descendants? In the kitchen, cooking or cleaning? No. In the stable tending the animals? Of course not! At the market running errands for their mother? No! Wake up and smell the goat's breath!

Nathan! Ezra! Get back here you sons of Satan or I shall rent out your rooms! Ooh! That's not a bad idea. For all I care you can sleep with the dogs.

I promise you I am not usually so crude. I am normally much more generous and compassionate. Why just this morning, a handsome young man from Galilee came to my door with a much too

MIRIAM, THE INNKEEPER'S WIFE

young wife sitting on scraggly old donkey. He asked for a room which I could not offer him. Then she got off the donkey and I realized his wife was not sick as I had assumed...the poor little thing was pregnant and obviously near her time. Suddenly the man got much less handsome. I thought, "That's all I need, a woman giving birth on our front step." Well, I told him they could stay in the stable if they wanted and I led them around to the back and helped get her settled. That poor little girl. I wonder what terrible sin she committed that God would send her the curse of children at such a tender age. Oh ... she has no idea what lies ahead for her. After all her hours of labor and all her love and sacrifice, she will finally hold her newborn child in her arms ... and he will throw up all over her. Then, as the child grows older, he will find more and more creative ways to keep throwing up on her.

Ezra! Nathan! Get in here this minute. There are floors to sweep, linens to change, dishes to wash, and animals to tend to! You have five minutes before I send your grandmother out to look for you! She has the nose of a bloodhound, the teeth of a lion, and the disposition of a hungry vulture. What a wonderful family I have. Oh ... the joys of motherhood. Oh ... the curse of children!

Elizabeth,
Mary's Cousin

Scripture reference- Luke 1:5-45

Children, they are a blessing of the Lord. There are very few things in life so precious as the innocence of a child ... the joy of a little one's laughter ... the warmth of his sloppy kisses ... or the moments you spend holding your own child asleep in your arms.

How long I had waited to know those feelings. I told myself it didn't matter, that we could be happy with or without children. "The sun will still rise and set, the tides will still wash in and out again, life will go on whether we are childless or overrun with descendants." That's what I told myself. But deep down, I knew the words were empty. Don't misunderstand. I realize that some couples may not need or even desire a family of their own, and many of those with large families often wish they could get rid of some they have. It isn't like we needed a child to make our house a home; Zacharias and I were quite happy. We were still a family, he and I, a family of two. But there was something inside me, deep inside me that told me, "Someday Elizabeth … someday, you will have a son." Every year it got a little harder to believe.

Then one day in the Temple, the angel Gabriel appeared to my husband, Zacharias. Gabriel, the one who stands in the presence of God, told him that I had already conceived and would soon deliver a son. I'm afraid he didn't receive the message very well; he laughed. Well, let's be honest, anyone would have done the same. A woman my age giving birth? Plenty of others laughed a good deal when they heard the news, I'm sure, and are still giggling under their breath. We had maintained our hopes for so long. But now? It would take a miracle.

When I heard the news, I laughed too! I danced around the room like a little girl! At last, I would bear a child. Those next months were glorious for me, even as the child's presence became more and more obvious. Most of my friends continued to laugh at me. I think they were afraid I had gone senile and was using pillows to keep up the illusion. However, through all the morning sickness,

ELIZABETH, MARY'S COUSIN

swelling feet, and near-total exhaustion, I was happier than ever. I found myself singing praises to God even when it took all my efforts just to get out of bed in the morning.

My cousin Mary came to visit me a few months before my son, John, was born. She didn't even have to tell me, as soon as she walked in the door, I knew she too was to have a child. For a moment, I must confess I was angry. How unfair that I had waited so long, prayed and cried God would give me a child and here stood Mary. She was barely old enough to conceive and as yet unmarried. I wanted to scold her, but instead a burst of joy came flowing up from within. John kicked within me as if he were dancing around in praise to God. Mary and I clung to each other and wept and prophesied for hours.

The poor girl needed a friend so badly and if truth be told, so did I. She too had been visited by Gabriel but couldn't understand why God would choose her for such an important role. I told her how God had taken care of us all these years, how He makes it all feel right. Even when others think you've done something awful, He can comfort your soul and give you the strength to stand in His truth. I urged her not to let the fears of friends and loved ones keep her from doing what God has declared she should do.

At our newborn son's brit, the priest questioned me about the child's name and urged me to change my mind. Zacharias bristled and wrote, "His name is JOHN" and handed the note to the priest. At that moment God forgave his disbelief. Suddenly, Zacharias sang God's praises so loudly people came running to see what was happening.

I can't tell you how proud I am of both my men, Zacharias and my son, John. God has answered my prayers and made us a family of three.

Mary too has given birth to a son whose name is Jesus. John arrived first, but God has spoken to me about Mary's son. There is something special about Him. Both boys are part of God's plans to redeem Israel.

Children, they are a blessing from God. Something deep inside tells me Israel's redemption has finally come.

Mary,
The Mother of Jesus

Scripture reference~ Luke Chapter Two

Neither Joseph nor I understood at the time what was happening to us, but we trusted God. He took care of us every step of the way. Joseph and I had been in love for years. Even as children, we talked about what our lives would be like when we were finally married. Not *if* but *when*. Gabriel had prepared me for what my parents and neighbors would think, but when I told Joseph ... well, it had never occurred to me that he would think that I had been unfaithful. I'd never seen such pain in his eyes. When he left that day, I was sure he would send me away until the baby was born. But the next morning, the joy was back in his eyes and he told me about his dream. Thank you, Gabriel! Thank you, God, for giving him back to me. I don't think I could have survived alone.

The trip from Nazareth to Bethlehem was especially hard. Joseph tried to get me to stay in Nazareth, but I refused. We had to be together, no matter what the cost. He warned me that the trip would be risky for me, but I begged him not to leave me alone when I was so close to giving birth. I remember riding on that donkey. My back was killing me, but I could never have made it on foot. Joseph could have made the trip so much more easily without me, but I was so scared. Neither of us had ever had children so we had no idea what to expect. We just had to keep our faith strong and pray that God would help us figure it all out ... and keep us safe. We prayed, "Lord, help us make it one more mile ... just one more mile!"

Once we reached Bethlehem, the Innkeeper, Micah, let us take refuge in his stable. He was so apologetic. Bless his heart, the census brought so many people into that tiny town there was not a bed to be found anywhere. Joseph and Micah worked long and hard to make me as comfortable as possible. Joseph was so sweet. He transformed that stable into a cozy little home for us.

Soon, the baby's cries pierced the night. I held my new-born son in my arms and counted his little toes and fingers. I breathed a long sigh of relief and wiped the tears and sweat from my eyes. Up to that moment, there had been no time to think ... or to imagine ... or to ponder, and I staggered under the weight of the thought. This baby ... is God's child. Jesus looked just like any other little baby, but He was so much more.

I remember several shepherds who came to the stable just after I had given birth. Micah started to shoo them away, but they told us about a choir of angels who had sent them to us to find the Messiah. It was so odd to see those rough men, total strangers, rejoicing over Jesus' arrival as if they were distant uncles. They told us about the prophecy the angels had given them. "Glory to God and Peace on Earth." Even in a place we had never been, God sent us a "family" to rejoice with us.

I remember feeling so terrible that we couldn't afford to treat Jesus like the King He was. But God knew our poverty and He still gave us His son to raise. I treasure those memories now. All of them. We learned to trust God completely ... daily. Otherwise, I could never have survived those last dark days when I had to watch my son suffer so. No one took my son's life. He offered it freely. And the cross didn't defeat Him. It was what God sent Him here for. When a group of ladies and I went to His tomb to embalm His body, an angel asked us why we were seeking the living among the dead!

Some may think of the cross as a symbol of death; I look upon it as a silent witness to the power of my Son's resurrection. His sacrifice brought peace into a world that didn't know what peace was. Jesus brought a new kind of peace ... the peace that only God can give. Because of Jesus, even in the midst of war and bloodshed, the Prince of Peace still reigns.

Mary Magdalene,
Delivered from Demons

Scripture reference- Mark 16:9-11

The first memory I have is of Him ... Jesus. Most of my youth is lost to me. I have a few hazy pictures in my mind that rise unbidden in my sleep, but a large part of my life was stolen from me by my masters.

When I was very young, I was kidnapped from my parents by a group of thieves who trade with caravan slavers. If I didn't submit quickly or completely enough to their demands, they would lock me in a dark cave for days with no food. They also kept me drugged most of the time with odd potions and devil brews. And they used me.

They discovered that under the influence of certain potions I could hear voices whispering things and I saw visions of what I assumed was yet to be. They were probably just hallucinations, but an amazing number of my prophecies actually came to pass, and my owners found a way to profit from my gift. People were willing to pay dearly for my predictions about their businesses or health, and at times they were allowed to buy more than my words.

Even now people are afraid of me or angry at the person I was. Not all of my visions proved reliable and sometimes they want me to pay for it. A woman recently recognized me and attacked me claiming I had promised her a son. Instead she gave birth to another daughter, her seventh. People call me a daughter of the devil, possessed by many demons. Others call me names I won't repeat and accuse me of being a lover of Roman soldiers. I can't remember enough to say that they're wrong.

As the story was told to me, my masters had me reading palms on the street the day I met Jesus. He grabbed me by my shoulders and declared, "Come out of her!" That is the first real memory I have. "Come out of her!" His voice echoed as from a thousand caverns and I felt screams and clawing from within. I could only see His eyes at first, which cut through the darkness of my soul. Then His face came into view ... and His smile. The warmth of His touch wrapped itself around me and gave me a new life. It was as if I were able to see the world for the first time.

When I finally found my tongue, I knelt at His feet and whimpered, "Master, I am your slave. Whatever you desire of me I will do." He took my hand in His and whispered, "You are a slave no more ... but my sister. Now stand up Mary, your new life awaits."

Salome, the mother of two of Jesus' disciples, has taken me into her home. She treats me as a daughter and is trying to teach me how to live on my own. These followers of Jesus are different from other religious scribes and teachers. They believe that all of us, even women, are equal in God's eyes. We are no longer slaves to sin or those who would control us with violence, but children of Jehovah God Himself. We do serve, but out of love and devotion, not fear or guilt. Salome said that all who come to God with repentant hearts ... all ... all will be forgiven. Slowly, I'm beginning to believe it.

I have wished for some time that I could do something for Jesus to prove my gratitude and devotion. I owe Him my life. I have nearly nothing of value except a small box of ointment that my masters used on me to make me appear younger. Salome says is quite expensive and rare. I had decided to sell it and give the money to Jesus but as I walked to the marketplace, something inside me told me to change my direction. Jesus is dining today at the home of a local tax collector who is almost as hated as I am. They will all be there for the meal. The priests who ignored my very existence. The "upright community leaders" many of whom once paid for my services. The Sadducees who call Jesus a son of the devil behind His back. I too shall join them. I have decided that in the presence of those who used me and condemn me for it, I will anoint the feet of Him who saved me.

Martha,
The Sister of Lazarus

Scripture reference- Luke 10:28-42, John 11:1-44

Tell me, have you heard about Jesus, the Miracle Man from Galilee? Yes, the one everyone is talking about! Would you like to meet Him? He just happens to be a dear friend of my family. He has stayed in our home hundreds of times and He said my fig-nut-grain cakes are heavenly! He and my brother, Lazarus, are as close as brothers ... and just between us ... I believe He is quite taken with my sister, Mary. Oh, He has never said so, at least not out loud, and Mary insists that their relationship is purely platonic, but just between us, I'm hearing wedding bells! Now don't you go and tell anyone ... not yet.

Now I'm not one to spread rumors you understand ... but one afternoon Jesus and Lazarus were engrossed in one of their deep religious discussions. Oh my goodness yes, my brother is quite the intellectual! No one in Bethlehem can keep up with him when he starts babbling on about the fine points of Jewish doctrine, or whatever it is that men talk about. Well, naturally I retired to the kitchen. After all, religion is a man's concern. I started to prepare dinner. I had this fabulous new recipe for pomegranate chicken. I was going to try it out on Jesus. He is always so complimentary, even when all I have in the house are a few loaves and fishes. Well, suddenly I realized that it was nearly dusk, and Mary hadn't even cleared away the dishes from lunch. That girl! I have told her and told her, "Mary, how can you expect to find a husband when you're so lax about your womanly responsibilities?" Well, you'll never guess where I found her! She had been sitting with the men all afternoon, making moon eyes at Jesus, hanging on His every word, pretending she understood what He was teaching! You realize of course that this is strictly between us. You mustn't tell a soul. I don't want Mary to get a reputation ... we have to get that girl a husband and soon!

MARTHA, THE SISTER OF LAZARUS

I finally cried out, "Mary! It's not healthy for a woman to study religion. You know what the Levites say. If we women learn too much our poor heads will explode." Jesus leapt to her defense and said that not only should Mary be allowed to stay but that I should listen as well. He actually said, "Dinner can wait!" Dinner can ... what?? Then I figured it all out. He must be smitten by her. Why else would he possibly want a woman around while He talks about God?

I declined His invitation and returned to the kitchen. Well, someone had to be sure that pomegranate chicken didn't burn.

Jesus is a bit unconventional in His behavior, but He certainly comes through when you need a miracle! I hear He has turned water into wine, healed lepers, given sight to blind men, and sent cripples leaping and running back to their homes. He always says that Jehovah God does these things, but I think He's just trying to be humble. But His greatest miracle of all, He saved for us ... well, technically I suppose for Lazarus, but Mary and I were right in the middle of it.

For some time, my brother had complained that he didn't feel well. It was hard to take him seriously; men are such babies when they get sick.

One little cough and they want you to wait on them hand and foot. One morning though, I knew something was seriously wrong when Lazarus couldn't even get out of bed. He is a lot of things, but he's not lazy. So, I sent for Jesus. I figured if He healed people He didn't even know, then He would surely want to heal His best friend. But days went by and He never replied to my messages. Mary said, "Martha, He'll be here soon. He won't fail us." But what if Lazarus dies? How will we live without a man in the household? What's to become of us?

The next morning, Lazarus died.

I had to take care of the funeral arrangements and hire the mourners myself. Mary is no good in a crisis. After the funeral was over, I finally let myself grieve. Until Mary burst in and said that Jesus was finally on His way. "Oh, He is, is He? Well, I'm going to give Him a piece of my mind!" I ran out and met Him on the road. "Where have you been? I thought you loved my brother! Well it's too late now! He's dead! Get out of here and leave us to mourn in private!"

Jesus wept. I'd never seen him do that before. In fact, I had never seen any man cry before. I didn't think they could. But I still don't know if He was crying because He felt guilty for arriving too late to save Lazarus ... or because I blamed Him for it.

Jesus strode to the tomb entrance and shouted, "Lazarus, come forth!" There were a few moments of awkward silence. Finally, we heard a few scratching noises, as if someone was dragging a heavy sack across the sand. Finally, we saw that it was Lazarus hobbling out into the sunlight. Jesus said, "Someone, help him unwrap his grave clothes." He turned and looked me straight in the eyes.

I said, "All right, all is forgiven." Then I went to help my brother.

I was never so happy to have been wrong about someone! The greatest miracle of all time and He did it for our family. What? Oh no, He knew I couldn't stay mad at Him very long anyway. After all, we're friends. And that's what friends do ... they forgive.

Bildah,
The Cross Woman

Scripture reference- Matthew 27:48

Most little girls want to be mommies when they grow up. Some dare to dream of becoming a female warrior or athlete. Others, from the time they are very young, seem to have their hearts set on being Queen, or at least looking like one. But as for me, I have always wanted to help dying people. Yes, you heard me correctly. Let me explain.

If a man is very sick and the family cannot ... or will not care for him, they call for me. I sit with those who are beyond medical help. I hold their hand, so they won't feel alone or deserted as they pass. Sometimes I sing to them or quote King David's psalms. Then, when their spirit has finally left the body, I close their eyes, wash their faces and wounds, straighten their hair, dress them nicely, and call for the family.

I also give drugged wine to condemned criminals at public executions. For crucifixions, I hoist it up in a sop tied to a spear. It doesn't stop their pain, but it reduces it somewhat. In my lifetime I have witnessed seven hundred forty-three passings ... more than half of which occurred at Roman executions. The Soldiers just call me "the Cross woman." I consider that a term of respect and even appreciation.

It's not that I enjoy watching people die. I have simply never felt the need to fear it. Somehow, I cannot see death as an ending, but as a kind of second birth. A child doesn't ask to be born, yet it happens, nonetheless. I've never met a sane person who wanted to die either, but neither process can be avoided ... only postponed. You cannot stop a baby from leaving the womb and you cannot keep a man from dying. But just as a mother holds her newborn to her breast to help make his entrance into our world more gentle and calm, I try to offer the same kindness as they leave us. I hold them and try to comfort them as they pass into a new life ... gently and with dignity.

I take pride in my work. After all these years one would expect me to be able to do my job as if it were any other everyday task, like making the bed

BILDAH, THE CROSS WOMAN

or sweeping the floor. But every time I watch someone pass from this world ... yes, each and every time I am filled with wonder. I ask myself the same questions over and over again. How does this happen? Where do they go? Are they at peace in their new world, or in hellish torment? Do they simply fall asleep or do they remember what happened to them here?

One might think I would have answers for these questions by now, but I am more convinced than ever that there are no answers to be found ... at least not among the living.

Today, I watched a Galilean die on a cross. The Romans say He was a heretic, that He claimed to be the only son of Jehovah. A mob of unsavory men circulated through the crowd paying people to shout, "Let Him be crucified." But, at His feet there were several women weeping uncontrollably, insisting on His innocence and begging the soldiers to spare His life. I felt the urge to join them, but I had three men to attend to ... not just one.

Two other men hung on crosses on either side of Him. They bit their lips and sneered at the crowd. They were fighting the pain, trying to ignore it. That was phase one. It normally lasts about two or three hours. Then next come pleas for mercy, which turn to curses and then finally the victim is exhausted and gives up the war. I watch the prisoners' faces closely to see when the wine will do them the most good. If given too early, it can weaken their resolve to breathe, but once the intense pain begins, the wine is of little comfort.

The man on the center cross, the Galilean, kept searching the sky and mumbling things I couldn't hear. Only occasionally would He look down at me, but I saw something in His eyes that I had never seen before from a dying man. He was worried about me. His eyes were asking, "Are you all right? I'm so sorry you have to see this." He was thinking about my pain rather than His own.

Toward the end, He said to one of the other thieves, "Today you will join me in paradise." Paradise. What a beautiful thought. It could have been the ramblings of a delirious man, although He never accepted any of the drugged wine. But I don't think so; I can't get that picture out of my mind, Paradise! In my mind's eye I can see the Galilean putting his arm around his co-sufferer and leading him through Heavenly gates into a glorious city, whose builder and maker is God. If only there is such a place, a paradise where people go when their earthly lives are over.

BILDAH, THE CROSS WOMAN

I think it may be true. I do! I believe it must be true. Thank you, Galilean. From this day forward, I will carry that picture in my mind ... and write it on my heart. Perhaps one day I too will join You ... in Paradise.

Zelda,
The Servant of Pilate

Original character not found in scripture

Can you feel it? Of course, you can feel it! Do you hear it? Of course, you can hear it! Listen with the ears of your soul. See with the eyes of your spirit guide. It is the heartbeat of the universe ... boom boom ... transcending ... boom boom ... Yommmmmm. Don't just sit there, chant with me! Yommmmm. You're not chanting with me! You will never be onnnnnne with the spirit realmmmmm until you hummmmmm the proper tonnnnnnne. I can see you know nothing of religion. You are as blind as my master, Pilate.

Wait a minute! I'm getting a message from the spirits. Shhhh! I'm trying to become one with the spirit realm, but its voice is so soft. The spirits must have a touch of laryngitis!

KEN LEE—VOICES FROM THE BIBLE

(Selecting a member of the audience) You madame! The spirits have told me that you were once frightened by a ... by a ... a ... fire breathing dragon when you were only ten years old. Am I right? No? Are you sure? Oh, I see more clearly now. It was not a dragon ... but an elephant who threw water at you when you were only *six* years old. Am I right? No? Hmmmm, now I see it clearly. You were nursed by a gorilla when you were only two years old. No? You were a baby! How would you know?

Never mind. I will sacrifice a rat to the gods for you and ask them to repair your memory. Do you have some incense on you? I go through a lot of it lately. Why? Did you just ask me why? I'll tell you why I sacrifice. Jupiter is red. Saturn refuses to enter his house and the moon is singing to the deafened sun, that's why! We are in the middle of a crisis people. Wake up and smell the hibiscus! Pagans. I'm talking to pagans.

The rhythm of the universe has been interrupted by this Galilean prisoner they call Jesus. The world is screeching to a halt. I can feel it in my bones ... no ... deeper than that ... I can feel it in my soul ... no ... deeper than that. I can feel it in my belly, my intestines, my spleen ... oh I'm making myself sick.

ZELDA, THE SERVANT OF PILATE

This Jesus must be a powerful wizard, the most powerful wizard of all time! I told Mistress Claudia, "Mistress," I said. I said, "Mistress," I said ... "Mistress," I said. All right I forgot what I said. But I told her to warn her husband, Master Pilate. He must have nothing to do with this just man!

Oh...I have suffered much because of Him. He walks through my dreams. First, He walked through my mind carrying a sword. Then He walked through my soul carrying a chicken. Then a fig cake. And a then a birthday cake and then ice cream and then I realized that I wasn't asleep at all. I was just hungry ... so I got up and ate a sandwich. But that first part was right. Better leave that water walker alone!

Master Pilate! All nature cries out against the death of an innocent man! You must wash your hands of him. Wash, Pilate, wash! Wash your hands of His innocent blood! Wash, Pilate, wash. You better wash them again for I can still see His blood! Seriously ... right around the fingernails. There! I think you got it! Wash, Pilate, wash.

Wait, I'm getting another message from the spirits! There is a man here ... a very handsome man ... Oh spirits are you sure you have the right room? Oh, you sir! *(selects a man in the room)* It must be

KEN LEE—VOICES FROM THE BIBLE

you of whom the spirits speak ... because all the other men are sooooo ugly! The spirits tell me that you have a mole on the little toe of your left foot! Am I right? No? Sure you do. Take off your shoe so I can see if you're lying. No, on second thought I don't have enough incense left for you to remove your shoe. And this room isn't well ventilated. Wait, the spirits now tell me you have a pimple on your knee. The spirits better make up their minds! Am I right? Do you have a pimple? No? Oh good, they can be really annoying! No I have it now. You once had a pimple on your face, didn't you? Am I right? No? Don't give me that! You did so! Next time, spirits, choose a man who is more honest.

But back to the story! I must consult with the wizards and seers of Turin, and the oracle of Delphi, to see if their power can stop this Galilean from turning the world on its ear! I fear that no earthly force can stop what Jesus has begun! The life force of our world has changed forever.

Oh Mars! Oh Milky Way! Oh Snickers! *O-kay* that's it, I'm obviously too hungry to prophecy. You'll have to catch me again after lunch.

A Mother's Prerogative

Original character not found in scripture

(Care must be given to keep the audience from knowing who is speaking until she identifies herself.)

The greatest curse a mother can have is to watch her son die. It's wrong. It's a violation of nature. The parent should die before her child. That's the way it should be.

That's what I told myself as I stood on the hillside of Golgotha staring up at three crosses. I still have no idea how my legs managed to support me. I was bone-tired and had cried till I had no more tears left. Yet somehow, I stood there, transfixed for hours … my eyes nailed to the cross along with Jesus.

I had tried for months to catch up to them, my son and his friends. It seemed like I was always a day or two behind them. By the time I managed to reach a town, they had already moved on and the crowds had gone home. But everywhere I went, people were talking about the miracles God had done through them. I heard men and women who had been dumb sing praises to Jesus, their Healer. I held the hands of lepers who had been completely healed and restored. I met a woman who had been demon-possessed and heard her talk about her deliverance. I watched children born lame running and playing.

My son had always been such a blessing to me, and of course I knew the day would come when I would have to share him. As I watched those children jumping and dancing around like that, I remembered my own little boy playing on Judean hillsides with his friends. I remember listening to him recite scripture for his papa, and then sneak an extra fig cake when he didn't think I was watching. I remember sitting all night watching him asleep on his mat, praying that his fever would break. He was so beautiful ... my son ... my hope.

A MOTHER'S PREROGATIVE

But as I stood in that crowd, watching Roman Soldiers kill an innocent man, my hopes were dying with Him. I saw her next to the cross, Mary the mother of Jesus. She was surrounded by women as she wept for her son and tried to keep her heart from bursting. I envied her. Yes, I envied her. For even though she was watching her child die, she knew the truth. She will always know that He was innocent ... that He had been murdered by villains, enemies of God. She will be able to heal, to find comfort in His teachings and the testimonies of those whose lives had been changed by His sacrifice.

However, my son ... my precious Judas ... the son I prayed for and loved ... he took his own life.

There are no answers, only questions. There was no chance to talk him out of it ... or to say goodbye one last time. No chance to caress his brow and tell him once again how much I loved him. Judas, why did you do this? Why? There are no enemies to hate, only an emptiness deep in my spirit ... a darkness that will always follow me.

Mary-Not-The-Mother

Original character not found in scripture

Have you heard the news? It's absolutely unbelievable! Well, I suppose it's not completely unbelievable, after all it really happened! So, it is believable ... I mean you should believe it because it's true. Only no one's going to believe it because it is so ... unbelievable!

Hi, my name is Mary. No, not Mary the Mother of Jesus! Do I look old enough to be the mother of a Messiah? I know her, Mother Mary that is, and some people say I look like I could be her daughter ... but just a little. Mary is a very popular name right now. There are Marys all over Jerusalem. Besides Mother Mary, there's Mary from Magdala, who comes from ... Magdala. And Fat Mary, only better not call her that to her face. And there's Tall

Mary who raises the roof when she's mad at her husband. And Big Mary who keeps rollin' down the river. Like I said, there are a lot of us Marys. So, everyone calls me Mary-Not-the-Mother!

That name bothered me at first ... Mary-NOT-the-Mother ... but then I realized they might have chosen something really bad ... like calling me by my father's name, Mephibosheth! Mary of Mephibosheth! Wow, that's a mouthful.

Come to think of it, why don't men have extra names? I mean Father is just "Mephibosheth" and Andrew is just "Andrew" and Peter is just "Peter," ... although I did hear one of his fishing buddies call him "Old Fishbreath" once. But why isn't John called "John of Zebedee"? Or James called "James of Alphaeus"? Or Thaddeus called Thaddeus of ... okay I have no idea where he came from.

Whoops! There I go again. How did I get started talking about names? I'm sorry, I get easily distracted. I start off talking about one thing and then I realize I've drifted off again. Like right now. What were we ... oh, that's right! I was about to tell you my unbelievable news! I mean my not so unbelievable news. Wait a minute. On second thought,

MARY-NOT-THE-MOTHER

maybe I shouldn't tell you. What if you don't believe me? Nobody ever believes me when I tell them good news!

I told Rebecca about the wedding in Cana, you know, how Jesus turned the water into wine, but did she believe me? Nooo! Then she hears it from Zadok and suddenly she throws her hands in the air and praises God.

And the day Jesus multiplied the loaves and fishes, I came running home to tell my mama, Mary of Moab, but would she believe me? Nooo! Then Andrew tells her the same thing and she's all, "Praise the Lord! How wonderful!"

And when I ran to tell Caiaphas the High Priest about how the crowd welcomed Jesus into Jerusalem riding on a donkey, he actually yelled at me and threw me out of the room. Can you believe it?

Okay, it happened again. Oh! My news! I haven't told you my news yet! It's unbelievable! But you had better believe me! This morning, I went with some of the other Marys to the tomb where we buried Jesus. Joseph of Arimathea donated it. Oh, how about that! Joseph of Arimathea ... I guess some men do have extra names. And Simon of Cyrene and John the Baptist! And here I am talking about names again! And just when I was getting to the good part.

Okay I'm just going to spit it right out ... but you better believe me. You promise you'll believe me? Nod your heads and say, "Yes Mary-not-the-Mother! We'll believe you!" *(After audience responds or fails to do so)* Okay that was just sad ... but I'm going to tell you anyway!

When we got to Jesus' tomb, what do you think we found? Go ahead, guess! You'll never ... what? That's right the tomb was empty. How did you know that? And we saw two ... that's amazing! Yes, they were angels. You must be clairvoyant! And guess what they told us ... that's right! Jesus is alive again!!! God raised Him from the dead! What's wrong with you people? It's like you already knew. Okay you promised you'd get excited! You bunch of deadheads!

Oh, I know who'll get excited for me! Blind Balthazar! Last time I told him some good news he jumped up and down like a madman for over an hour. Of course, the good news was that I had just found my pet cobra, crawling up his leg.

Oh, look there he is! Hey Balthazar, do you want to hear something unbelievable?

Boy! For a blind man he can run pretty fast.

Ken Lee as Joseph the Carpenter

ABOUT THE AUTHOR

Rev. Kenneth W. Lee has been part of the St. Louis and St. Charles community for nearly fifty years. He has been associated with the St. Charles County Home Educators for at least twenty of those years, having taught at Dayspring, Pillar Foundation, MBU, and has offered private voice lessons and special summer music camps for St Charles County students. He is an active member of Saturday Writers in St. Peters.

Ken is ordained with the Assemblies of God and has served as minister since 1972, and as Pastor at Lakecrest AG Church in Wentzville from 2006 till his retirement in 2019. Ken earned a BA in Speech with a minor in voice from Evangel College, an MAT in Communications from Webster University, and completed the course work for an MA in Theatre at SIUE.

For 26 years, Rev. Lee traveled as a full-time Drama Evangelist performing in 40 states, four foreign countries, churches of over 30 denominations (for as few as ten and as many as 6000 people), on Christian television networks and radio broadcasts as well as National Conferences for the Assemblies of God, General Baptists, and the CITA. He has also been featured artist for a number of Youth Conferences around the country. He has recorded four albums of original music as well as three drama videos (Portrait of the Man, The Roman, and Day of the Cross) all of which are available on YouTube. He now does a weekly Facebook posting called "Ken's Korner" as well as weekly postings of him singing old hymns.

Mr. Lee has performed as guest actor/soloist with Bob Pickett and the St Louis Concert Choir as well as an occasional role for MBU. In 2000, Ken was fortunate enough to star with Todd Farley in a production of "David" for Thurlow Spurr, Cam Floria and CMI and the Continentals which performed in the Citadel of David in Jerusalem.

Ken was married to his college sweetheart Dr. Sharon Shockley Lee from 1972 until her death in 2005, and he has two adult sons, Justin and Jared, and three beautiful granddaughters, Samantha, Jessica, and Aria.

His first novel, *One Size Fits All*, is now available on Amazon. Ken is currently publishing all of his original plays in a series of anthologies titled *Voices from the Bible*. Volume One includes all of the plays that built Ken's career as well as a number of monologues written for his students, both male and female. Be sure to watch for Ken's new devotional book titled, *Seasons in the Son,* which should be released by the end of 2020.

YouTube Performance Links:

"The Roman"
https://www.youtube.com/watch?v=_IiGrfPHmr0

"Day of the Cross"
https://www.youtube.com/watch?v=Y4desa1gY3k

"Portrait of the Man"
https://www.youtube.com/watch?v=B7jr8VYR_ZY

Please feel free to perform any of these scripts free of royalties as often as God will allow.